NORTH AFRICA TRAVEL, NUMBER 1

GW00504084

NORTH AFRICA TRAVEL

NUMBER 1

edited by Barnaby Rogerson

SICKLE MOON BOOKS

North Africa Travel, number 1, first published in October 2001

First published by Sickle Moon Books, part of Eland Publishing Ltd,
61, Exmouth Market, Clerkenwell, London EC1R 4QL. Published in
association with the Society for Libyan Studies, founded in 1969.
The Society for Libyan Studies is a British Institute Abroad funded
by the British Academy. Its aims are to encourage and co-ordinate
the activities of British Scholars in Libya
covering as wide a range of interests as possible.

ISBN 1-900209-19-5

Cover design by bk design.

Cover photograph of the custodian of the great mosque at Gao
by Barnaby Rogerson

Typesetting and text layout by Antony Gray to a bk design
Printed in Great Britain by Antony Rowe Ltd
Bumper's Farm, Chippenham, Wiltshire

CONTENTS

INTRODUCTION

North Africa Travel is an annual collection of travel-writing from North Africa and the Sahara. Its geographical frontiers stretch from the Atlantic shores to the banks of Nile, from the Mediterranean coast to the banks of the Niger. It is intended to concentrate on the core territories of the Maghreb: Morocco, Mauritania, Algeria, Tunisia and Libya while acknowledging that influences from Egypt, Andalucia, Sicily and the countries of the Sahel and Sudan are vital aspects of this region.

North Africa Travel welcomes contributions from scholars but it does not intend to become an university journal. Its aim is to bridge rather than widen the existing gap between journalists and academics, between travel-writers and archaeologists, between the specialists and interested travellers.

North Africa Travel is to be written in clear English. This is both a limitation in that the dominant languages of scholarship in North Africa are Arabic, French, Spanish and Italian but also a welcome oppurtunity to present new translations.

North Africa travel will especially concern itself with the narratives of explorers, the evidence of early trade and pilgrimmage routes and historical documentation. It is also interested in the whole compass of North African travel be it classic literature or film, photography or documentary news footage, or just excerpts from memoirs, diaries, travelogues, sketchbooks and postcards. It is also hoped that as well as looking at the European perception of North Africa it will also be able to reveal North African perceptions of Europe.

In addition North Africa Travel also aspires to be of use to the traveller. It will have a noticeboard for listing small hotels, good travel-agents, for bookshops, restaurants and unusual monuments. All correspondence may be addressed to North Africal Travel, c/o Sickle Moon

Books, Third Floor, 61 Exmouth Market, Clerkenwell, London EC1R 4QL. No payment can be offered to contributors though they will receive three copies on publication and can buy further issues at half price. This first issue has only been made possible by the generous and disinterested support of the Society for Libyan Studies.

Barnaby Rogerson

STRIDING FORWARDS,
LOOKING BACK
ANTHONY SATTINS IN ESSAOUIRA

M. FREDERIC DAMGAARD first entered the walled city of Essaouira twenty-five years ago, when Yusuf Islam was still called Cat Stevens and when Jimi Hendrix and a host of other sixties 'scene' people were hanging out, getting stoned on good, plentiful *kif*. The hippies went away, but M. Damgaard stayed and several years later opened an art gallery in a cool and cavernous house near the city gate. A first-time visitor to Essaouira stepping into the Galerie Damgaard before seeing anything else in town is likely to be amazed. The vibrant oil colours dazzle the eye and the force with which they have been applied to board (canvas being rare and expensive) provokes all sorts of questions. The images were unlike anything I had seen or imagined elsewhere in Morocco and I was curious to know from where the inspiration had come. M Damgaard directed me towards the streets, along the quays, into the souks and cafes of this seductive town.

A row of palm trees lines the road opposite the gallery, casting elegant shadows against the rust-red walls of the inner town. Old Souiries in jellabas rest in these shadows in the heat of the day. Later, when it is cooler, women covered by their haiks chat beneath the walls while their children play on the short-barrelled cannons which guard the high keyhole entrance to the old town. This, it is clear, isn't just any old town. Beyond the palm trees, Essaouira's defences are easily breached. For some this is a problem. It means that suddenly you leave the rest of Morocco behind and arrive in the heart of a town whose soul belongs to African slaves, ruthless pirates, Jewish traders, British tea merchants and a host of other exotic characters. When you pass through the gate, you step into the story of Mogador.

Old Mogador was just a name to me, but it wasn't long before people were fleshing it out, telling stories about the origins of the town. Even in antiquity there was a settlement around the good anchorage, protected by a string of small islands. In the sixteenth-century there was also a commanding Portuguese fort, but Mogador as we see it wasn't begun until the 1760s when Sultan Sidi Mohammed decided to punish the rebellious people of Agadir by creating a new port that would take away their business. According to legend and two guide books, a French architect called Theodore Cornut, whom the sultan happened to be holding captive, was offered his freedom in return for designing the town. The reality is a little more prosaic: Cornut was paid well for his work and a contemporary noted that he was shown all the honours due to 'an engineer of the kings of England and France.'

Whatever the truth, Cornut's stone bastions and fairytale fortifications have protected Essaouira's inhabitants for two centuries and still guard some of their secrets. But there is more to Essaouira than this. Sultan Sidi Mohammed moved the Jews from Agadir and in Mogador their community prospered, producing several important families, including a Mr Disraeli, father of the Victorian prime minister. Christians were lured with lower taxes and by the 19th century Mogador had become a great trading centre and a crossroads of cultures. Known as 'the port of Timbuktu', in its souks Africans, Arabs and Europeans traded slaves, gold and other African 'commodities' for European cloth, Chinese tea and metal teapots made in Manchester, now as essential a part of life in Morocco as sunshine and music.

During my first night in Essaouira, asleep in an old stone house with whitewashed walls and blue-washed shutters, I dreamed of a painting I had seen in the gallery. The image, by an artist called Mohammed Tabal, was of a man striding forwards, looking back. In Europe Tabal's work has been called naive and primitive, but such labels are misleading, suggesting links with artistic movements elsewhere. Tabal's ancestors arrived with trade caravans from black Africa, his father was a gnaoui, a mystic musician – the name T'bal signifies a large drum – and as much as anything else within the walls, Tabal's paintings belong to Essaouira. Like the city, there is a story attached to them: the one of the man walking, with his sardines, his tagine pot, truck, mosque, arched entrances and palm trees, is unmistakably a tale of the town.

In the morning, foreigners arrived from Agadir to do what they have been doing for the past two hundred years, shopping in the souks, lunching by the sea and listening to gnaoua play their music. They didn't stay long, but me, I preferred to do as the man in the painting and carry on walking, looking for clues to help me understand something of the secretive nature of the town.

Each morning I walked in the souks, still extensive though most of the Jews and European traders have gone, through alleys of brilliant fabrics, of silver, amber and necklaces of heavy stones brought from the desert. Each day I found something new – shoemakers weaving raffia, chameleons and a menagerie of dried birds or animals to cure everything from broken toes to broken hearts, pottery as brown as the earth, as green as the gardens of paradise, desperate townspeople selling their spare trousers or the shirts off their backs in the second-hand souk . . . To walk there was to indulge my senses. It was also a good way of seeing people, of meeting some of them and hearing their stories. What's more, it was easy to do – this isn't Marrakech or Tangier and, perhaps because there have always been foreigners in Essaouira, there is less hassle and few 'guides' promoting their uncles' shops or special tours of the ramparts.

Beneath the ramparts, even without a guide, I found Essaouira's woodcarvers, continuing to earn themselves a good reputation and, for some, also a good living. Marquetry is what the town is now best known for and the alleys outside the dim workrooms are scented with the resin of thuja-wood, a rich, dark timber from which the craftsmen make boxes and bowls, picture frames and tables, inlaying them with creamy lemon-wood, with iridescent mother-of-pearl or darker acacia and ebony. It is an old craft and an apprenticeship in Essaouira's workshops used to be a lengthy, tradition-ridden affair, starting with the fetching and carrying and ending, so many years later, at the top of the hierarchy, designing, overseeing and inlaying. But better education and sharper ambition are bringing changes: while old M. Boumzzourh, a master ebonist, carves frames and boxes in his small workshop, his son Abdel Nasser has a large showroom nearby, selling designer thuja-wood furniture to the likes of Yves Saint-Laurent.

For most of my stay in Essaouira the air was still, the ocean calm, the sky an unblemished blue. Late in the afternoon I used to walk along the kilometres of beach, watching football matches, courting couples and families out for the air, wondering why Essaouira's beach front hasn't been 'developed' like Agadir's in the south. On my last day the wind picked up and then I had my answer. Surfers don't call Essaouira 'Windy city Africa' for nothing: with a minimum of gale force 4 for 250 days a year, what is paradise on the waves can be purgatory on the beach.

On my last afternoon I stayed in town and was glad I did. For a magical hour, as the sun lowered itself over the ocean and the last tour coaches headed back to Agadir, Essaouira's strongest colours came out and allowed me to pick up the pieces of Tabal's painting. In the old port, fishermen unloaded their catch under the silent gaze of their wives, the quays busy with porters whose faces suggested the different races that have sailed in over the centuries. Elsewhere others gutted fish, baited hooks or loaded crates onto trucks, passing beggars hoping for a handout. Back in town the souvenir shops were being locked up, the souks still busy, the ramparts closed, a solitary game of beach football running into extra time, sea gulls settling on Cornut's battlements, women lounging on low walls and garden benches, a few men strolling into the Grand Mosque, young girls managing to flirt beneath their veils. It seemed as if the whole town had come out to breathe the cooler air and savour a moment's rest at the end of the day.

Then suddenly it was over. Darkness fell and, like everyone else in town, I stopped walking and looked for a place to sit and eat. By the following morning, the colours in Essaouira's gallery were no longer a surprise and before leaving town, I went to buy Tabal's painting. It cost more money than I had to spend and it wasn't easy to carry on the plane, but it was a small price to pay for the memory of such a magical place, striding forwards, looking back, taking care of its heritage along the way.

THE GNAWA BROTHERHOOD OF MUSICIANS

JANE LOVELESS

GNAWA are an esoteric brotherhood of healer musicians to be found all over Morocco. They are descendants of slaves imported into the country from the Western Sudanese empire from the fifteenth century onwards .

There are many groups of Gnawa in Marrakech and also in Essaouira. This coastal port, formally known as Mogador by its Portuguese colonists, was once a major port of entry for slaves from Timbuktou who were sold in its souks until well into the twentieth century. Nowadays, Essaouira is host to a thriving Gnawa community.

Like blues musicians from the Southern states of America, the Gnawa lamented the hardship of their lives in song. Today the tradition lives on with a strong spiritual emphasis – blending the beliefs of their ancestors with the theology of Islam.

Their music reflects the emotions of their forebears and their ceremonies have an essentially therapeutic function. The songs invoke and refer to supernatural entities as well as Allah, Mohammed and Islamic saints.

I have had a long-standing relationship with the Gnawa of Essaouira since my first visit in the nineteen seventies, and so when Western therapy failed to help me through a severe depression, I went in search of their help. Known for their healing powers, both physical and psychological, they enacted for me a ritual *lila* .

The evening began at the well in Diabet, a small village close to Essaouira. The Gnawa, beating large drums (*t'bol*) and clacking iron castanets (*qarqaba*), chanted and danced their way to the house where the ceremony was to take place. On our way, previously abandoned-looking whitewashed houses suddenly produced large numbers of men, women and children who joined the procession.

A striking-looking woman with kohl-rimmed eyes stood at the doorway of the house holding a lighted candle in each hand. She led us to an open courtyard to a crescendo of drum beating. Her name was Arbouche and she was the group's *mahkadma* . Her job was manifold. She was to tend the Gnawa and myself for the duration of the night, both in the ritualistic requirements and exercising her culinary skills. She had prepared a delicious chicken and olive cous cous which we ate in appreciative silence. The villagers who had followed us entered the courtyard, squatting and leaning against the walls waiting patiently for the music to begin. Arbouche cleared away the remains of the meal and brought mint tea. While we drank it, I watched her in the doorway of the kitchen laying out a tray bearing incense, dates and milk, all essential ingredients for the ritual which was about to get under way.

As the Gnawa fetched their instruments and began to play, she brought in a smouldering brazier and a large bundle of brightly coloured cloths which she placed in front of the musicians. The deep bass of the three-stringed *guenbri* and the counter-rhythms of the four sets of *qarqabsw* castanets rose above the voices of the musicians as they chanted to Allah and the saints, opening up the house to the spirits. They each had a dance to perform, whirling, somersaulting and jumping with an energy verging on the ecstatic. More villagers were crowding at the door, summoned by the hypnotic strains which rose from the courtyard into the starlit night. At about midnight, they stopped for a break and more mint tea.

Half an hour later the trance or *m'luk* began. This was when I would find out if the Gnawa would heal me. The rhythms of the *guenbri* were mesmeric. Arbouche pulled out a white lacy robe from the pile of cloths and started dancing, throwing a few pieces of incense on the brazier. She inhaled deeply from it, covered her head with a coloured cloth and picked up a large knife with which she repeatedly sawed at her arms and legs. Not a mark could be seen as I gazed in fascinated horror. The song drew to a close and another rhythm began. She slipped on a black robe, fetched a bundle of lighted candles and danced with them, holding them under her chin and against her skin. There are seven spirits summoned by the Gnawa, each symbolised by a colour appropriate to its character. Arbouche danced through the two blue spirits, representing the sea and the sky.

Then a new song began and I felt myself being drawn irresistibly towards the musicians, all Anglo-Saxon reticence having abandoned me. The dangerous red spirit Sidi Hamou had taken possession of my body. Arbouche draped a red cloth over my head and wafted the brazier of incense under my nose. I danced until I dropped and was taken to recover in a corner. A honey-covered finger was rubbed across my lips. I sat watching the green and yellow spirit dances come and go until finally the night drew to a close. Dawn was colouring the village as I opened the door of the house and looked out to sea. The Englishwoman who had walked into the courtyard the previous evening was very different from the person who emerged that morning – I felt reborn by the experience.

The night described above happened in 1993. The following year I bought a house in Essaouira where I now live and let two flats to mainly English tourists. I began to manage the group of Gnawa and have sent them all over Europe and the US. In 1998, together with two other people I started the now well-established Essaouira Gnawa Festival which takes place each year in June.

Originally written for the Hafla Music Village programme 1994 and amended in September 2000.

NORTH AFRICAN MUSIC
MARK HUDSON

A WOMAN, not three feet away, is going into a trance – stamping heavily, her torso rocking to the rhythm of iron clappers and a booming bass lute. As she collapses to her hands and knees, the clapping and the surging anthemic singing fall away, and there's just the sub-bass thrumming of the lute, twisting through what sounds like some far-out modern jazz solo, as though the instrument were somehow conducting and controlling the woman's trance. She begins to shudder and moan, and people rush to pull her from the room.

We're in a village outside Marrakesh, and this is the music of the Gnawa – the descendants of black slaves, who are called upon all over Morocco, to purify houses after death and to cast evil spirits from the mentally ill.

Western artists as diverse as 'Sheltering Sky' author Paul Bowles, left field New York producer Bill Laswell and jazzmen Randy Weston and Pharoah Sanders, have looked to Gnawa as a means of entering dark and elemental realms. At a time when the concept of 'trance' is endlessly and glibly invoked in relation to Western dance sounds, Gnawa music can prove an unnervingly intense experience, even through your domestic CD player.

I'm here with U-Cef, a London-based Moroccan drummer and deejay, at a lilla, a ceremony for the propitiation of the spirits, on the occasion of the Prophet's birthday. The overhead lighting in the turquoise-painted room is muted by incense smoke, the women seated round the walls adding syncopated clapping and their own fervent nasal singing as the musicians take it in turns to dance, leaping and whirling with a great stave strung with cowries, which keeps whizzing inches from my face.

Long before India and the hippy trail, Morocco provided a springboard into the exotic right on Europe's doorstep. As Westerners from Cecil Beaton and Joe Orton to William Burroughs and the Rolling Stones came here in search of easy drugs and risky sex, so Moroccan sounds fed into Western pop. Brian Jones's legendary recordings of the wailing oboes of the Master Musicians of Jajouka, a Berber village in the Rif mountains, were a World Music album decades before the event, while Led Zeppelin's Page and Plant have been blending Moroccan strings with hard rock since the seventies.

Over the last year or so, there's been a revival of interest in the region. Rai, the explosive Algerian dance music, whose digitalised rhythms, strident neo-Islamic vocals and message of youthful rebellion dominate the North African scene from the émigré communities of Paris and Marseilles to the depths of the Sahara, has excited Western listeners and musicians since the mid-eighties. The top stars have recently pushed through to a wider audience, with the charismatic Khaled's million-selling 'Aicha', and his rival Cheb Mami performing on Sting's 'Desert Rose'.

But the current wave of Western interest considers the region from a much broader perspective: looking at the myriad styles that fed into rai – Jewish crooners and cantors, Arabic country blues divas and the classical music of Moorish Andalusia – and at even older traditions, rooted in the semi-pantheistic culture of the indigenous Berber people, which blend remarkably easily with Western dance music.

'You can put Moroccan rhythms with anything – drum'n'bass, speed garage, house – and it works,' says U-Cef, who has made his own intriguing fusion of Moroccan sounds and cutting-edge London grooves, and who appears at the Barbican Centre as part of the 'African Roots and Shoots' season. 'Most Moroccan rhythms are loops – just like the digital loops we use in dance music. They just run into each, round and round, to take you to an ecstatic high.'

We find evidence of this later in our journey, in Casablanca, Morocco's biggest city and the capital of its music industry. Created by the French, the downtown area with its pavement cafes and art deco apartment blocks gives an impression of burgeoning affluence and buzzing commercial activity. But turning off the palm-lined boulevards, you step into an insanitary backstreet world that combines medieval street commerce with a very modern sense of unease. Tough-looking kids sprawl on parked cars, people stumble past – out-of-it on a lot more than the local *kif*.

By a hole-in-the-wall autospares outlet we meet Morocco's leading rap outfit, a couple of amiable youths in baseball caps, who are keen to chat with us in a high-fiving Bronx-English. You would assume they were desperate to jettison the last vestiges of their own culture, yet they call their group Dar Gnawa – the House of Gnawa – and they use gnawa rhythms to underpin their Arabic rapping.

'Gnawa music is something we've grown up with,' says one of them, Naima. 'It comes from black Africa, but it's something that every Moroccan, whether rich or poor, can relate to – deep down. So we're telling the world that we're Moroccan – and we're also African.'

The railway into Casablanca is lined with mile after mile of earth and corrugated iron shanties. The city's rapid and chaotic growth has given rise to extraordinary musical forms like chaabi, a politicised urban folk that greatly influenced Algerian rai. But dropping in on a middle class dinner party, we're assured there's nothing musically interesting happening in the city – the young people only want techno and Whitney Houston . . . Unless of course we count cheikhat.

The cheikhat – 'ladies' – are a traditional subculture of female entertainers, who in the transposition to the urban world have become inextricably associated with low-life. Like the Algerian folk diva Cheikha Remitti, the so-called old Grandmother of Rai, the cheikhat smoke, drink and sing about sex in the frankest terms . . . But to hear this music you have to be prepared to stay up late.

Along Casablanca's mist-laden corniches are any number of dodgy, overpriced 'Oriental Cabaret' joints, with vomit swilling on the toilet floors and rowdy young hookers shaking their mini-skirted loins on stage. We try several, all with the same line-up of pan-Arab synthesizer band, Egyptian-style crooners and a spot of belly dancing – and all at brain-splitting volume. We won't find anything of the remotest integrity here.

Then at two-thirty precisely, the lights go down, a trio of drummers set up a loping beat for a searing rustic violin, and a large man in a white gown and a demure-looking, rather pretty woman take the stage. Demure-looking until she starts singing – bellowing into the microphone as though she's got a grudge against it, alternating Islamic-sounding exhortations and sexual grunting, in a rasping whiskey growl, while the man responds in a hoarse woman's wail.

We've not only found one of the roots of rai, but a phenomenon that tells the story of much of the world's most exciting music – of the collision of traditional styles in the melting pot of the big city. But rather than being commercialised and digitalised for the world market, cheikhat has remained an underground people's music.

After two numbers, the club suddenly closes. As the punters stagger for the doors, I try to interview the singers. But he isn't interested and she seems distracted – to say the least. What, I wonder, do her family make of her singing this kind of music? She shrugs. She's putting two children through university – and she leans to whisper in U-Cef's ear. 'You have to give her another hundred dirhams,' he says.

Back at the Gnawa ceremony outside Marrekesh, it's time to eat. As we seat ourselves with the other men round a great tagine of lamb and olives, an old woman goes into trance, her son cradling her, as her frail body is shaken by violent spasms. She's part of the family who have called the event. Is it for her benefit – to drive out some malignant spirit? Or are we here for that robust-looking woman in her thirties, in the headscarf and the surprisingly fashionable glasses – the one who was the first to go into trance? No one has told us, and it doesn't seem polite to ask.

We came here by a circuitous route, with two members of B'Net Houariyet, a Berber's women's group, whose raw and powerful music was one of the hits of the 1998 WOMAD festival, and who U-Cef and I both greatly admire. Amina – lively and in her late thirties – and Fatma – ample, with henna-stained hands – are both extremely warm and friendly. But they don't look like the women I saw at WOMAD. Are they the same group? 'Of course,' says U-Cef. He's sure? He shrugs. 'Pretty sure.'

I feel a shiver of excitement as Amina, Fatma and their friends begin beating on drums, tambourines and what looks like a steel hubcap, their throaty exultant voices falling into an endless re-echoing round. Whether or not these are the women I saw at WOMAD, the music has the same blood-stirring rawness, the same Homeric sense of grounding in ancient rock and earth. As women perform hip-twitching dances back and forth across the room, U-Cef learns that these are not the women who went to Angleterre, but the ones who went to Belgique. 'It doesn't matter,' he says. B'Net Houariyet – 'girls' music' from the Houara region – is, apparently, a style, not a group.

Finally, the doors are closed, everyone settles themselves and the booming pulse of the lute – the *sintir* – and the smoke of incense again fill the room. It is time for the event to start. Start? It's nearly two in the morning. We've been here for hours.

The rhythms of the iron castanets begin to build, and with them an atmosphere of fervour and expectation. A round, chuckly woman who earlier gave us her business card – 'Breaker of Curses' – is one of the first to start trembling. Then Amina throws herself before the bowl of smouldering incense, inhaling deeply. 'From now on,' says U-Cef, 'things will become very trancy.'

EXTRACTS FROM THE ESSAOUIRA JOURNAL OF JANE LOVELESS

29th October 1999

THE RAIN, which began unusually early this year, has stopped and the more familiar blue skies returned. My neighbours are cleaning their doorsteps and playing loud Arabic music which is threatening to damage my brain. I have a theory that most people are deaf in this town. Televisions and radios are always turned up to full volume. Saîd, my neighbour tells me that Moroccan women are constantly fearful and that turning up the volume reassures them. I decided this morning to draw up a list of pros and cons relating to life here as opposed to living in England. The reason for doing this is that I seem to spend a lot of time complaining about things here and then over breakfast today I was reading last Monday's Guardian. I was appalled at what is going on in my homeland, which I think of with such nostalgia and fondness. How many times have I said to Moroccans 'this would never happen in my country, where everything works efficiently'. Where does this idea spring from? Have I had an inordinately sheltered life? Probably. And my memory perhaps plays tricks on me. I feel very relieved not to be spending the Millennium in London. No one even thinks about it here. It will be during Ramadan and that takes precedence over anything else that might be happening in the world.

Mina and I have created a small office space in my bedroom. Not the ideal place aesthetically but it's the only choice and I have the advantage of having the telephone on the table alongside the computer and printer. We have put the table behind the door, under the mirror. Mina thought it would be useful so that I could work and look at myself in the mirror. She found the idea very amusing, particularly when I expressed horror at the thought of seeing myself so often. I thought that in reality I wouldn't look up but of course I do every time I stop to think. As a result

I've started to pick at my face, something I have barely done since I was a teenager. I must try to find another place to hang the mirror.

I could hear dripping water this morning when I was having breakfast. I traced it to the lavatory of the studio which was leaking into my living room. There was an English couple up there last week and they had both been ill with the usual tummy bug. They had mentioned that they were afraid that they had blocked the loo with paper and I had given them a plunger to clear it with. It obviously hasn't worked. I shall try to make it go away with willpower. The thought of trying to find a competent plumber defeats me. The memory of my last plumbing experience is still too fresh in my mind. There had been a leak in the first-floor bathroom and I had been expecting tenants the following day. I had also bought a thuya wood lavatory seat which needed fitting, holes drilling and washers fixing. I had asked Mustapha to go and find a plumber and he had reappeared after twenty minutes with a man carrying a small bag of tools. This had looked promising. I hung around while he had seen to the leak (dollop of cement, much beloved by all workmen here) and I had shown him exactly where to fix the washers on the new seat. Three on the underside and the fourth at the front of the inside of the lid. I have to admit that I had concentrated mostly on the positioning of the three former ones, adding only that the fourth was needed so that the lid wouldn't crack the seat if someone dropped it down heavily (which is what had happened previously and which was why I was having to start again). At this point I had had to go out to see to an electricity problem in a friend's house. I had a man from the electricity board walk round the house with me and pointed out a live wire, split, hanging out of the wall near a water heater.

'That looks dangerous' I said.

'Ah oui, madame' he agreed, getting a small kitchen knife and a roll of Sellotape out of his bag. Unhesitatingly he cut the wires down to where the outer casing joined them, and bound them tightly together with the Sellotape. The mains, fortunately, was turned off. This was a man employed by the national electricity board and he was binding the live and neutral wires together. I got him out of the house as fast as I could, and ran back home to fetch my pliers, penknife and insulating tape. I could hear the plumber talking to Mustapha as he worked fixing the seat so I returned to my friend's house to split and bind the wires separately before the light faded. By the time I arrived home the job had been done and both the plumber and Mustapha had left. I went to inspect the seat. The lid was up and right in the middle at the front of the seat was the fourth, three-quarters of an inch thick washer, proudly screwed in. Incredulously I wondered how anyone could have thought of putting it there. When Mustapha came in later I asked 'Look at this. Does it look normal to you? Is this what we have in the bathroom upstairs?' He shrugged and said he thought it looked okay. 'You don't think it just might be a bit inconvenient there? And unhygienic? And TOTALLY RIDICU-LOUS?' I finished on a slightly hysterical note. 'Alright, I'll move it later if you like,' he humoured me. I had already gone to fetch a screwdriver and did it myself feeling yet again mystified by this strange country I live in.

I have just had Saîd round to help me with the current leak. After examining it carefully from above and below we decided that some white cement will seal the source of the leak which emanated from the lavatory waste pipe. I asked Mina to clean the bathroom first so that we could work in there and leave the cement to dry. Saîd set to work, making a neat job of it. I came downstairs to answer the phone, Saîd walked out of the bathroom and before he had time to stop her, Mina rushed in with a bucket of water and all the cementing which he had so painstakingly done was washed down the drain. Mina, like all Moroccan women, loves throwing buckets of water around. You see it cascading down the stairs in houses and all floors are built with a slight slope towards a drainage hole. It was all I could do when I was having my kitchen put in to present the builders from making 'la pente' on the work surfaces. It's surprising in a country where water is so short.

The Bearded Madman who arrives in my street every morning between seven and eight o'clock and remains either hunched in a door-way or standing facing the rampart wall until late at night, with the occasional interlude when he sets fire to small piles of wood, was offered a small job today by Abdeladi who works in his brother's thuya gallery on the corner. As I passed he was handing a cloth to the B.M. indicating that he wanted him to dust his motorbike. The B.M. is so filthy himself that I should think that more dust would fall off him than he could hope to wipe off with the small cloth he was given. Full marks though to Abdeladi for employing the B.M. instead of giving him the wide berth I do in my prissy way. I cannot but admire the way that social outcasts are com-pletely accepted here. Is it Islam?

1st November

It's much cooler today, and misty. Its as if God knows the date. I went to the bank this morning, squeezing past the handful of women beggars who take up residence outside the gates during opening hours. I have hardly ever seen anyone give them anything. It seems to me that one goes to the bank either to put money in or to take it out. Either way the sums involved are invariably in notes so it is extremely hopeful of them to imagine that someone is going to hand them anything. I'm always mystified at the general shortage of small change. This is a country where people go and buy just enough tea, sugar and mint for one pot so very few people spend more than a few dirhams at a time. Yet when I go out to buy some bread the shopkeeper sometimes doesn't even have change for ten dirhams. A hundred dirham note often has caused such problems that I have been given credit all day in the various places where I shop. I'm glad that I'm trusted by all the shopkeepers but it involves retracing my steps the moment I eventually manage to get some change. Where is all the small change? Is it like the low tides and all goes somewhere else? Do the beggars have piles and piles of it stashed under their beds? The bank was very crowded, being Monday. Turbaned Berbers who look as though they haven't got two rials to rub together, pull several thousand dirhams out of the hoods of their djellabas to put into their bulging bank accounts. The Berbers are generally hard working and good businessmen. They tend to see further than the end of their noses, realising that making a small profit every day will eventually enable them to buy a second and third shop. Arabs on the whole seem to have a live-for-the-day attitude. Make as much money today, spend it at fast as you can, and never mind if your hapless customer never comes back to your shop again. My theory is that somewhere Islam is behind it.

Hafid, a woodworker, typifies the attitude of 'here by the grace of God I am alive today'. I had bumped into him in the street one day. He was looking unhappy again, having regained his cheerfulness a few months after his wife's accident. This had been a dreadful event: Hafid loved going round the second-hand markets and had quite a collection of bric-à-brac in his home. One of his finds was an old metal framed table lamp which he had wired up himself. The day of the accident had in fact been the celebration of his son's circumcision. Members of the family were coming in from the countryside, preparations for the feast had been going on for days. Hafid had gone out very early and his wife set to work washing the floors, which of course meant throwing quantities of water everywhere. Like all the houses here, there were no windows on the ground floor where they lived, so barefoot and wet-handed she switched on the table lamp. She died instantly. The guests arrived to find they were attending a funeral instead of a circumcision. I had seen Hafid a few days later. 'I'm so sorry to hear about your wife,' I said. 'It's not serious,' he had replied. Not serious? Was this a form of politeness? I had gone to see Desmond, an Englishman who lives here and is a friend of his. We discussed the fact that although Hafid was shocked and upset at his wife's death, he didn't in any way hold himself to blame for it. It was God's will, not his, Hafid's responsibility. So when I saw him months later looking so glum I asked him what the matter was.

'My uncle has died.' he told me.

'Was it an accident?' I inquired cautiously. 'No.'

'Had he been ill?'

'No.'

'Was he an old man?'

'No.'

'So why did he die?'

'It was God's will,' he replied with resignation and humility.

I remember feeling angry and puzzled and had arrived home to find Mustapha and his friend Azedinne preparing a tajine. I told them about my conversation with Hafid, finishing with an exasperated 'How can he accept that? Why doesn't he demand to know the reason?' Both Mustapha and his friend replied simultaneously 'But its normal. We could go to bed tonight and not wake up in the morning. God might decide to take us'. The longer I live here the less I understand.

A WEDDING AT FEZ

ANTHONY GLADSTONE-THOMPSON

'HE WHO does not travel knows not the value of man.' We may not attain Ibn Battuta's enlightenment, but Fez for a long weekend together is a milestone.'

Leila was wearing a grey corduroy suit over a rollneck pullover, though the day promised to be fine. She turned to Jeremy, appealing for his confirmation.

'Presumably Ibn Battuta didn't have a tyrannical father watching his every move.'

'Mine can't bother us this time: he's dancing attendance on the Sultan in Rabat.'

Wary of inquisitive gendarmes, they were taking minor roads. However, a police roadblock had been set up by Rommani's Ifriqiya garage, and they found themselves being questioned.

'And where could an Englishman be taking a young Moroccan woman?'

'To her father's house in Fez.'

'You will encounter problems. Berber tribesmen have come down from the mountains and surrounded the city. They wish to remind the nation that it's their Independence Day, too.'

They drove on through oak and thuja forests towards Oulmès.

'What are the Berbers up to, Leila?'

'Making people take notice, to reinforce their influence and nationhood. When Rabat talks of a united realm, their fear is that means essentially an Arab one.'

'I hope they don't upset our plans. Where exactly is your house?'

'It's in Fez El Bali as opposed to New Fez, which is only thirteenth century.'

They were nearing El Hajeb. Watched by egrets, men were hoeing the ground; the autumn fields and orchards evoked a pastoral idyll Leo Africanus would have recognised.

'You remembered the key?'

'Of course. Fatima wouldn't open the door however loudly we banged.'

Jeremy was taken aback. 'Surely no one else's going to be there?'

'Fatima wouldn't betray us; anyway, she's deaf and dumb. She's been a fixture since my grandfather's time, when she entered the household as a slave.' Leila burst out laughing. 'I've shocked you now! Slavery has long been abolished, but Fatima's always refused to retire. She has no use for money, as we provide everything and house her.'

They entered Fez, crossing the French-built town; faded and dormant, it seemed the remaining Europeans were in hibernation. They approached the western ramparts at an angle along Boulevard des Saadiens. Now the tawny battlements swung northeast, and they would need to turn right. The junction, however, was blocked by police.

'Tourists?' The gendarme was too harassed to observe Leila properly. 'The whole medina's closed off. You'll have to turn round, or take the Meknes road.'

'Monsieur – please listen. We're expected at my father's house, in the Attarine district. Surely there's one gate into Fez El Bali open?'

'You don't trust my judgement, Mademoiselle? The city's encircled, and the Berbers are obstructing every approach. In western dress, it wouldn't be safe even to try.'

'If we can reach the Palais Jamaï Hotel, I can telephone my father. You can be sure he'd be very grateful.'

'Is that so?' The gendarme nodded slowly: Leila must be one of many pleading special circumstances. 'All right. The mass of tribesmen are on the south and east sides: you can proceed, but keep clear of the medina.'

They followed the ramparts, beneath which dozens of lorries were parked, garlanded with fairy lights and palm fronds. Soon the Kasbah des Cherada loomed before them.

'We'd normally fork right here for Bab Boujeloud, but just look at that crowd. Better follow the panoramic road.'

Snatches of drum-playing could be heard above the hubbub, and the sound of guns being fired into the air. Armed men were milling about with Berber casualness and colour, yet the scene radiated menace, as of a race awakened to its power.

'It's like the fifties, when the Berbers last held Fez in a stranglehold. They'd never allow an infidel like you to pass.'

The deserted road now climbed away from the ramparts. Nestling in its hollow, Fez had never spilled out from the protection of its millennial walls; the myriad square rooftops, all at different heights, gleamed like an Atlas amethyst. Eventually a gentle descent led them towards the northernmost edge of the medina. A dozen gendarmerie jeeps lined the road keeping the approach to the Palais Jamai open, and they were waved through.

The foyer was choked with tourists. Instead of revelling in the opportunity to witness a historic Berber gathering, the visitors were fussing over the upset to their plans; the manager's gestures confirmed his powerlessness in the matter. Jeremy and Leila squeezed through to the terrace, and ordered drinks.

It was pleasantly warm, and the milky blue and violet light did honour to the gardens of the former palace. The hushed atmosphere momentarily belied the Arab city immediately beyond the walls. Now its seething proximity made itself felt with shouts, animal cries, hammering, bells, evidence of incessant activity and vitality; abruptly, there came the muezzin's call to prayers, his forceful summons taken up by all the city's mosques, near and far, overlapping each other in a blaze of resonance.

A cat looked up from its washing as Leila stirred the sugary lees of her *citron pressé*.

'Are you ready?'

The gardens descended in a series of *riads* surrounded by opulent suites. Glancing up at the tiny swifts banking among the palms, they followed a walkway edged with rosemary, then strolled under a pergola, awed visitors to this harbinger of paradise. Their route zigzaged round a pavilion into another courtyard. A maid was sorting laundry; Leila, wishing to proceed unobserved, pretended to inspect an orange tree.

'On the other side of that wall lies the medina.'

'It's a dead end, Leila. We can hardly climb over.'

An archway led to a service area, where flies circled in a shaft of sunlight. Leila ducked into a lean-to; sidestepping gardening paraphernalia, she pulled open a narrow steel door set in the back wall. Seven feet of musty tunnel in the thickness of the ramparts lay before them. Leila tugged at the chest-high bolt and the outer door grated open, revealing an alley.

We'd better go the long way round to avoid Bab Guissa. I hope tribesmen aren't roaming within the medina.'

The narrow pathway twisted and kinked in a downhill direction. They passed numerous turns and sombre passageways, some mere recesses piled with putrid rubbish, and at one point followed an ill-lit tunnel beneath a building. They hugged the walls, giving way to donkeys intent on their footing on the uncertain ground, the loads chafing the beasts' backs. In the evening light the occasional stare from the throng of passers-by flitted over them, neither curious, nor acrimonious, nor collusive.

Now they joined a busier street lined with poky workshops: bookbinders, slipper makers, bowstring-lathe turners, perfumers, assailing them with the blatant odours of their trades.

'The Kairaouine lies directly to our left, though with all the shops built against its walls, you'd hardly know. Nearly there now.'

After turning off and proceeding uphill, Leila stopped at a studded door with a green-tiled canopy. Jeremy helped her unlock it, noticing one knocker at chest height and another much higher for mounted visitors. A ninety-degree turn through a pitch-black passage brought them into a courtyard, with an empty basin at its centre. Ranges of shuttered doors and windows surrounded them.

'I'd rather not confront Fatima until morning. Her room's on the roof, at the back, so she won't see us.' Leila moved towards a lofty, one-storey building, and opened the double doors set behind the horseshoe arch. Four cube-shaped alcoves, furnished with rugs and couches divided up by plump cushions, gave off the hall. Each *salon marocain* had a small window, set into the wall above the white and bottle-green *zellige* tiling.

'This pavilion is only meant for entertaining. The back doors lead to a small garden, with its own gate into the medina.' Leila tossed her bag down, and came towards him. 'The daring lovers are safe now, in the heart of Fez. What a day – '

Jeremy brushed her cheek with his lips and smoothed her hair. Her dark eyes reflected a spangle of light from the brass wall lamps.

' – though nothing compared to what I had in mind for tomorrow.' Leila hesitated. When we've found somewhere to eat, I'll tell you more.'

A carpet emporium by day, at night the once-grand house near Bou Inania Medersa became a restaurant. The candlelit, split-level layout, partitioned with moucharaby screens, enabled them to choose a table away from a group of British tourists.

There was no menu, but their hitherto overlooked appetites responded to the waiter's description of *chorba* soup and *briouats*, served with a bottle of Guerrouane. When the chicken with olives was placed between them, Jeremy followed Leila's lead, ignoring the unmatched cutlery and using his fingers and the plentiful bread.

'Well?' he eventually asked.

Leila ducked her head before raising it to gaze at him.

'Do you like dressing up?' She plunged on enthusiastically: 'I hope so. There's everything we need at the house. But I'd better start at the beginning.

'You remember it was only after Independence that we moved to Casablanca, so all my infant memories crystallise here. My brother and I used to play hide-and-seek through the interconnecting rooms and around the alcoves in our pavilion; my favourite hiding-places were the old wardrobes, among the carefully preserved finery of past generations. My brother would find me easily, because I couldn't resist dressing up. Then, extravagantly attired in caftans, I would squat cross-legged with the women while they gossiped begging Fatima to decorate my hands with *harqus* painting.'

'That painstaking, crisscross pattern? I thought it was a tattoo.'

'It's not permanent. Fatima used her own mixture of charcoal and oil. Another treat was listening to my grandfather's tales of the Sale rovers, Bou Hamra's revolt, the fate of the Jamai brothers, whose palace became the hotel, and the splendours of the Saadians.'

Leila laid her hand on Jeremy's. 'Besides the wardrobes, there was a chest whose contents I was forbidden to touch: the gorgeous wedding apparel worn by generations of family brides. Wrapped in tissue paper and locked away from the light, those robes and their accoutrements became a source of fantasy and longing for the day they would be mine.'

Leila was trying to make herself heard above the cabaret. The Moroccan entertainers had inveigled the tourists, still holding their cigarettes, into a mockery of a traditional dance.

'Unless I marry some puppet of my father's, my lifelong dream will not be realised and I shall never wear the magnificent costume of a Fassi bride. So tomorrow, Jeremy, let's dress up and conduct our own wedding ceremony.'

After dinner they strolled warily towards Bab Boujeloud; outside, campfires were burning and musicians were playing boisterously. They walked back to their medina hideaway, past stalls lit by hissing gas lamps, tiled fountains, dark passages and barred doors. The discreet garden entrance, which Jeremy would never have found on his own, yielded to a concerted shove. The pavilion lights were still on, and a golden glow suffused the citrus trees and the sunken path. Eventually they fell asleep at right angles to each other on the sweet-smelling Moroccan divans.

The Berbers had maintained their blockade, and the Palais Jamai management had responded to its clients' plight by laying on a *mechoui*.

After buying *sfinge* doughnuts that morning, they had opened the shutters, and Fatima soon appeared to investigate. A well-built, black woman with an unlined face, she embraced Leila with a huge grin and rumbles of laughter. Jeremy came forward, his presence causing the briefest surprise before he, too, was seized in a massive hug. Fatima fetched coffee and watched them eat, mimicking the recent highlights of her life with prodigious energy.

'Her cousin is suffering from some terrible swelling, which defies medical prognosis,' Leila interpreted. 'It hasn't rained in her *bled*, and the cows have developed rickets. Meanwhile, the Berbers have been made welcome, but everyone's hoping they don't stay too long. And she thinks you're very good-looking.'

Afterwards, Fatima opened the residential wing. Apart from the costume chest and *marfár* display shelves, the furniture was French in heavy gilt. Jeremy was allowed a peep into Leila's old bedroom, with its innocent furnishings and nostalgic air of a rarely-used retreat.

Their door into the hotel grounds had not been rebolted, and they had seated themselves on the terrace for lunch. Leila proposed Moroccan salads and *b'stila* before the roast lamb.

'Morocco has been called a cold country with a warm sun: let's soak it up while we can if we're to spend the afternoon indoors.'

'What shall I be wearing?'

'In keeping with Fassi tradition you'll wear white, but first I want you to try a splendid courtier's garb of my grandfather's: his master the young Sultan Abd El Aziz loved costumes and play-acting when his stern vizier Bou Ahmed wasn't looking. Let's just have fruit to finish with; there'll be *cornes de gazelles* to accompany the celebrations.'

Fatima threw open the chest to reveal silks and brocades glinting under their tissue wrapping, and carried the spoils to the *salon marocain*, hooking back the double doors. She had readily grasped from Leila's scant, graceful gestures what was afoot.

Leila's choice for Jeremy took longer to find. 'Change in the next alcove – no need to be bashful in front of Fatima: she understands the hang of such costumes and the intricacies of their fastenings. Better pack your own clothes into your bag, otherwise the place'll look like a school changing room.'

Fatima laid out his attire in deliberate order, pointing first to a white shirt. Jeremy struggled to pull his head through the embroidered neckband. Next he put on a pair of voluminous, dark-blue *seroual* breeches, finishing just below the knee and drawn in at the waist with a cord; Fatima buttoned the pleated bands on his bare calves. There were two waistcoats: the first was in matching royal blue edged with gold thread. Fatima secured each of the twenty caftan-like fastenings before passing a crimson belt ten inches wide round his midriff. The second waistcoat was more generously cut, and billowed open to reveal the belt beneath. Finally he slipped on the heavily embroidered jacket, reminiscent of a toreador's suit of lights, with sleeves slit from the elbow to the cuffs.

Fatima lifted a rolled turban with red felt underlay from its wooden mould, and set it halfway down Jeremy's forehead, while he slipped his bare feet into a pair of crimson *babouches*, the back folded down under his heel.

'My Janissary, my master!' Leila exclaimed. 'Will my lord walk with me; you're ready now to do the Sultan's bidding: hold his bridle, or conduct an ambassador into his presence.'

'Or claim my Cleopatra's hand in marriage?'

'You look so dashing! It's the finest *keswa del mahsour* imaginable. Now we must change into our wedding attire. Fatima will help with the drape and folds of your *ksa* and *selham* cloak. Then she must devote her energies to me.'

Fatima handed him a bulky woollen blanket, an embroidered satchel on a white silk cord and a cloak with a large, tasselled hood.

'Take off your clothes for Fatima to put away. She'll begin arraigning me while you practise draping your *ksa*. Open it out, bring one end over your shoulder and tuck it into your waistband; drape the rest behind you, let it fall in a loop, then bring it over your head and down, so that the fringed end just brushes the floor. Gather up the loose cloth, and fold the surplus forward over your left shoulder.'

The procedure was less daunting than it sounded. Although the *ksa* was twenty feet long, once he had secured one end and passed the cloth over his head it became quite manageable. The satchel was obviously supposed to go round his neck. He took a few steps, the satchel bouncing on his hip.

In her alcove, Leila was sitting astride several cushions piled on the divan, her bare legs swinging clear of the floor. 'It's too tight, Jeremy, you look like a mummy. Try again. The *shkara* satchel will hang better if there's some weight in it.'

Presumably the noblemen who once donned the *ksa* had a valet to assist. Jeremy's keys and wallet were strewn on the divan, and he stuffed them into the satchel.

Leila was monitoring his second attempt. 'Good! Now take the fringed end and throw it over your shoulder. Fatima will add the finishing touches.'

Fatima slung the satchel diagonally across his right shoulder and tightened the cord. She adjusted the cloth where it passed over his turban, and fussed with the *ksa*'s drape. Finally, she twitched the cape-like *selham* over his shoulders, the creamy wool contrasting with the *ksa*, and smoothed the hood down. The bulky outfit and height gained from the turban lent him the not-to-be-trifled-with appearance of a Fassi patrician.

He walked about outside, attempting a lordly gait, until Fatima finally summoned the impatient bridegroom back to the pavilion. His darling was caparisoned rather than dressed in sumptuous brocades and jewellery, a transcendent, fairytale demeanour enhancing her familiar beauty. Leila must be siting cross-legged on the pile of cushions, though her feet and hands were hidden beneath the tent-like cascade of loose, padded coverings. Crowned with a diadem, she regarded him with bashful composure, her eyes enhanced with kohl.

Fatima, now wearing a garnet-coloured caftan, stood nearby, her jubilation undisguised.

Jeremy was at a loss for words. He attempted to plant a kiss, but his turban snagged on the diadem.

'Do you have to stay up there?'

'It's physically impossible to walk around. Tradition requires the *arousa* to display her bridal finery for women friends to admire. No pecks on the cheek: the full make-up, which would take hours, resembles the embroidery on your previous costume.

'Your lifelong ambition has been stunningly realised.'

'Look how intricate it is. Underneath, I'm wearing a caftan of the palest blue-green, the colour of dawn. Then come two stoles in gold brocade, reaching to the ground – look.'

Leila's hand emerged from below, grasping the stoles. 'They're covered in turn by the embroidered cushions on my lap and these red and gold brocade squares, which are pinned to the hanging behind me – hence my inability to move. When I need to be carried around, a sumptuous caftan in white, gold and pale green is thrown over my shoulders. Nothing is buttoned or fastened, to keep evil jinn at bay.

'The headband under the diadem anchors these mesh-like strands of tiny pearls, interwoven with black braid to make it seem my hair is plaited with them. Finally, five bellows-shaped filigree pendants are pinned to this velvet-covered plastron.'

'Could I ever afford the endowment you must command?'

'A man apparelled as you are would have no difficulty. I readily declare you an honorary Moroccan, and fit to be my husband.'

The clink of glasses announced Fatima's return, bearing a vast tea tray.

'Then how and when can we marry in the eyes of the world?'

They both heard the unmistakable creak of the front door. Fear surged and clutched him; as he turned towards the sound, Leila signalled frantically to Fatima. The latter's hand flew to her mouth, then she hurried across the courtyard towards the blind corner where the unexpected arrival would emerge, blocking Jeremy's view.

'My father!' Leila's voice was an unrecognisable gasp. 'Quick – escape into the medina. Not the back door – he'll see you. Through that window.'

Jeremy leaped on the couch and threw open the casement. Unable to get his leg over the sill, he thrust his shoulders through the narrow opening and levered his body out. He tumbled into a bush, whose springiness broke his fall; he struggled to his feet and pushed the window closed. A moment later a man's voice could be heard, its tone questioning, then angry and strident. Leila stammered some reply, and he shouted again; Leila screamed, then there was silence.

Jeremy hurried to the gate. He remembered the knack, lifting the door by its bolt to prevent it scraping; a second later, he found himself alone in the alley. He leaned against the wall, his chest pounding. For a wild moment he considered storming back to confront her father, making him understand they intended to marry. He took a deep breath. So long as he was not seen, she could claim she was dressing up alone with Fatima. He adjusted the *ksa* and straightened his turban.

He suddenly remembered his holdall. He had left it by the divan; his clothes, shoes, everything he had brought to Fez was stuffed inside as Leila had instructed. He frantically checked the satchel: at least he had his keys, wallet and identity card. Now a girl carrying a tray of unbaked loaves on her head came round the corner. Jeremy hastily turned his face to the wall. Leila's honorary Moroccan had become an impostor and a fugitive.

He could not afford to linger: at any moment her father might find the holdall and come in pursuit. He strode off, tugging at the *ksa* where it framed his face to leave his features in shadow. If he followed what was little more than a passageway, he would shortly emerge into a much busier alley. Turning left here yesterday had brought them into Rue Talaa Seghira, which led to Bab Bouieloud. Turning right would set him on the tortuous, and much longer, route to Palais Jamaï.

He could hardly cross the hotel foyer without causing a stir, if indeed he could find the way; better make for Bab Boujeloud and commandeer a taxi. He was confident he would soon reach the first landmark, the tiny Moroccan bakehouse that must be the girl's destination. He walked briskly, his eyes lowered, occasionally stopping to ram his feet back into his *babouches.* He passed the baker's, and soon reached a small square with a withered tree; he fell in close behind a string of mules laden with bleeding sheep's heads.

Once in seething Rue Talaa Seghira, it should have been easier to proceed unnoticed, but now he felt a sharp tug on the hood's tassel: a boy was pointing and laughing. He hurried on. Approaching the Medersa, he glanced back; the lad was now leading a troop of children, chanting and jeering. Then a passing Fassi dressed in an everyday version of his own attire, berated the children, causing them to run off.

The crowd was much denser approaching the gateway. Craning over the heads, Jeremy saw the police were manning a barrier to keep townsfolk and tribesmen apart. An idea occurred to him, and he turned back towards the mosque. In a nearby street, he found the hammam that he was expecting. He extracted a ten-dirham note; he would hand it to the attendant and be given change, avoiding the need to speak Arabic. Some Moroccan in the bathhouse would gladly exchange his cheap European shirt and trousers for such a rich set of clothes. Then he would engage a guide to lead him back to the hotel.

The sour-faced woman attendant cried out, blocking his way. As he retreated, two matronly figures entered, with every sign of being welcome. Jeremy swore to himself: the baths were exclusively for women in the afternoon.

Two boys, crouching in a pit recessed into the wall, stared at him as they fed wood into the hammam's boiler. He doubled his pace, conscious that the route he was now taking had bypassed the main Boujeloud gate. Fifty yards further on, the alley widened into a square. A dozen tribesmen with knives at their waists and staves were arguing with some towns-people. Over their heads, Jeremy glimpsed a row of *petit taxis*.

He shuffled forward until his path was barred, then deftly side-stepped the Berber. Dodging between parked cars he ran for the taxi rank, conscious that he was being pursued. Beckoning vigorously, a quick-witted taxi-driver opened the rear door and leaped behind the wheel. Jeremy felt a restraining grip on his shoulder; he pulled himself free, abandoning the *selham* in the man's hand. As he slipped into the taxi, the driver accelerated away.

The man was pleased with himself, and began joking in Arabic.

Jeremy attempted a guttural laugh. 'Palais Jamaï!' he ordered.

The driver spoke again, but in the absence of a reply stared at him in the mirror, frowning all the way to the hotel.

Once he had paid him off, Jeremy settled himself awkwardly in his car, and prepared to drive to Casablanca. He gritted his teeth and clenched the steering wheel resigned to forsaking his darling, their wedding in disarray and their union unconsummated.

At the Meknes road checkpoint, the gendarmes had been re-inforced by soldiers in gaiters. Sirens wailing and lights flashing, a formation of motorcyclists appeared, leading a procession of vehicles: men in dark glasses, army officers in gold braid, and then the Sultan himself in a Mercedes Pullman, followed by communications vehicles and an ambulance.

A gendarme was eyeing Jeremy, and having concluded his saluting, approached the car.

'Are you French or Moroccan, Monsieur?'

Jeremy understood the man's Arabic, but gave his nationality in French.

The officer's frown intensified. 'Why are you dressed thus? A little fun at our expense on Morocco's Independence Day, perhaps?'

'It's for a fancy dress party. I chose it because it's so handsome.'

'You can hardly manage the pedals. Take the *ksa* off, Monsieur.'

'May I ask what brings the Sultan to Fez?'

'He has been meeting his Berber subjects in the Mechouar, and accepting their expressions of loyalty. Tonight he will feast with their leaders to celebrate Independence. Tomorrow, the tribes will depart to their *bled*, *in sha'Allah*.'

THREE'S A CROWD

Personal and professional rivalry behind the Borno Mission, 1822–1825

JAMIE BRUCE-LOCKHART

FROM the very start, an apparent lack of foresight, combined with laxity in communication within and between the organising and sponsoring institutions, put at risk the welfare, safety and success of the British government's Mission to Borno, and led to a serious, and potentially dangerous, clash of personalities and interests among the expedition's members.

The Borno Mission was the fourth attempt by the British government after the Napoleonic wars to explore the interior of Africa between the Guinea coast and the Mediterranean littoral, and to determine the final course of the Niger river. Its main concerns were geographical and scientific; while there was naturally a commercial interest, there were as yet no specific abolitionist or imperialist aims. The plan was based on information received from George Lyon, following his return from a similar attempt between 1818 and 1819 – an expedition which had had to be aborted on the death in Murzuq of its leader, Captain Joseph Ritchie. The new Mission would set out from Tripoli, with the support of the British Consul, Colonel Hanmer Warrington, and cross the Sahara to the central Sudan under the protection of the Regent of Tripoli, Yusuf Pasha Karamanli. The moving force behind the project, and its original organiser, was Sir John Barrow, Second Secretary at the Admiralty. Its official, and financial, sponsor was the Colonial Office, under the Colonial Secretary, Earl Bathurst.

Barrow was a powerful administrator in a department of state much concerned to enhance British presence and prestige overseas. A former explorer himself, he also had a personal goal. In the spirit of the period of enlightenment, Barrow was actively engaged in the advancement of scientific knowledge and the encouragement of geographical

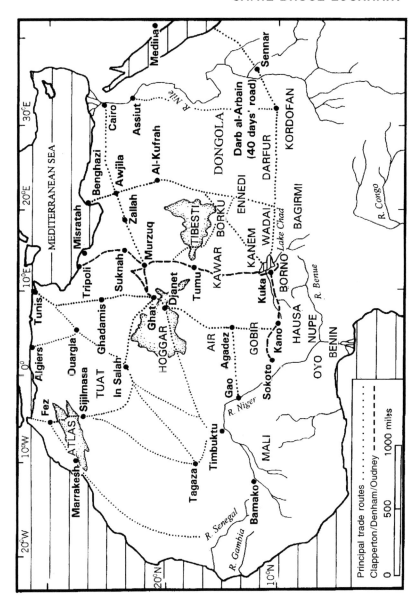

discovery. With respect to Africa, a particular hobby horse of his was the final course of the great River Niger, which he firmly believed to terminate in the Nile. Bathurst, on the other hand, was less personally interested in African exploration. He was also something of an absentee landlord from his department at this period; and the mood of parliament and government after the wars was one of colonial retrenchment not expansion.

Three officers were appointed to the Mission: Dr Walter Oudney, Major Dixon Denham and Lieutenant Hugh Clapperton, RN. The first to be approached was Walter Oudney. A former assistant surgeon in the Royal Navy, Oudney had turned to the study of natural sciences and was making a name as a botanist at Edinburgh University. He came from a modest background – his father had been an artisan – and lived at home with his mother and two sisters. He was quiet, serious and withdrawn, and (something he apparently kept from Barrow) was suffering from consumption. Barrow had chanced to visit Edinburgh, to receive an honorary degree, not long after he had learnt of the results of the Ritchie-Lyon mission, and evidently asked his University friends to recommend someone suitable to lead a new expedition of scientific enquiry into the interior of Africa. Walter Oudney's name was suggested, put forward by Barrow to the Colonial Office in November 1820, and duly accepted.

At this juncture, the plan proposed by Barrow and accepted by Henry Goulburn, the Under-Secretary at the Colonial Office, was for a two-man mission. Thus, when it transpired that Warrington, though an eager supporter of the Saharan missions, would not himself participate, Oudney was invited to nominate a companion to accompany him on the journey. He chose Hugh Clapperton, a fellow Scot, a neighbour and good friend. An enterprising naval lieutenant on half pay, Clapperton, who had been born and brought up in the small town of Annan in Dumfriesshire, was somewhat at a loose end in Edinburgh. He was a tough, much travelled and independent-minded man, of a forceful and rather difficult character. Barrow, keen to have a member of the Royal Navy in the Mission, accepted Clapperton, who was to assist Oudney in the work of exploration and also manage the expedition and its logistics. After some delays, this appointment was confirmed by the Colonial Office in July 1821.

In March 1821, however, a third name had been thrown into the ring, that of Major Dixon Denham. Well-bred, well-read and well-connected, Denham became a solicitor, and then purchased a commission in the English Army, serving in the Peninsular War as an ADC to one of the generals. In peacetime he had gone on to join the staff at the Military Academy at Sandhurst. Inspired by Lyon's accounts of his Saharan travels, Denham obtained a personal introduction to Lord Bathurst, to whom he put forward ideas on a possible route of travel through Fezzan to Timbuktu and the Niger. Denham's recent contact, on academic military matters, with the all-powerful Duke of Wellington no doubt prospered his application. The Colonial Secretary was rather impressed by this articulate and personable officer, and duly had him officially appointed, in June 1821, to take charge of the proposed new mission into the interior.

The records do not reveal when, or in what terms, Goulburn informed Barrow – or indeed Oudney, and hence Clapperton – about the addition of a third officer and the leading role apparently envisaged for him. Goulburn, embarrassed perhaps by his political master's imposition of Denham on the mission and no doubt overburdened with other administrative duties in his rapidly expanding department, may have been less than explicit and possibly failed to coordinate adequately with the Admiralty. Barrow for his part, having achieved his primary objectives – funding of the expedition and direct involvement of naval personnel – may well have been unconcerned about the addition of a third officer, and thus similarly failed either to foresee the consequences or take remedial action. One detects on both sides a whiff of arrant carelessness. The seeds of confusion, strife and much unhappiness had been well and truly sown in an undertaking where there were now no clear lines of command and responsibility. From the moment of their first meeting, in London in August 1821, it was evident that the mission's complement contained all the ingredients for a serious clash of personalities.

Clapperton and Oudney on one side and Denham on the other, viewed the execution of the Mission very differently, reflecting experience in armed services with quite diverse traditions. The two factions were also fundamentally at variance in their goals for exploration, Denham believing the Niger to flow eastward to join the Nile, while the two Scotsmen, following the thesis of their fellow-countryman, James McQueen, were convinced that the Niger terminated in a delta in the

Bights of Benin and Biafra. Furthermore, any prospect of constructive cooperation during the Mission was threatened by differences of social class, background and outlook, combined with serious incompatibilities of character. Clapperton and Oudney left London first, on 3 September 1821, receiving official, written instructions only the night before they took ship at Falmouth. Their instructions brought no clarification as to the lines of command. Issued in a hurry by the Colonial Office, with apparently little, if any, consultation with Barrow, they were merely a rewrite of those given to Ritchie and Lyon three years earlier. The question of overall command had been fudged. The Colonial Office had attempted to resolve matters by giving the Mission two parallel objectives. They named Oudney as Vice-Consul designate in Borno, and put Denham in charge of the work of exploration, with Clapperton attached to Denham. Oudney's responsibility for scientific tasks was ignored and he deeply resented his removal from the work of exploration. Clapperton, who had volunteered expressly to accompany Oudney, was infuriated to find himself under the orders of an interloper – an interloper who, to add insult to injury, was junior to himself in rank.

Denham had already compounded this offence by attempting to blame his Scottish partners for delaying the start to the expedition – it was essential to ensure travel across the Sahara in the cool, dry winter months. This accusation was quite unjust, Oudney having written repeatedly to Barrow to urge an early start for that very reason. On the journey out to Tripoli, Oudney and Clapperton were to have engaged the services of a naval carpenter at the Malta Dockyard to join the Mission. However, the local authorities knew nothing of the project and, lacking official instructions, were powerless to assist. That did not stop Denham roundly accusing his travelling companions of rank incompetence, when he later arrived in Tripoli, bringing with him from Malta a ship's carpenter named William Hillman.

When Oudney and Clapperton arrived in Tripoli in October 1821, Warrington might have helped resolve some of the difficulties, but the genial, bumbling Consul General, instinctively avoiding anything as uncomfortable as arbitration, only made matters worse. Asked by Oudney to clarify London's ambiguous instructions, Warrington's written reply gave him to understand that he, Oudney, remained in overall command of the expedition, 'to Conduct this Interesting and Important Mission'. And on

Denham's arrival in November, Warrington similarly allowed him to continue in the belief that he had overall charge of the Mission. Warrington did, however, attach an additional officer to the Mission: John Tyrhwitt, an easy-going, robust, twenty-five-year old former Naval midshipman whom he had taken on, as a favour to a family friend, in the Consulate.

There were delays in Tripoli as negotiations continued with Yusuf Pasha Karamanli concerning the provision of an escort across the Sahara – by subordinates the Regent did not trust through territory he did not control – and in January the travellers decided to wait no longer but to proceed to Fezzan, where an armed force was promised to be made available shortly. Tyrrwhit, whom Warrington hoped to have appointed as Vice-Consul in Murzuq to keep open a line of communication and supply, accompanied them as a supernumerary. Denham, an articulate, experienced and skilled political diplomatist, did rather well in dealings with Yusuf Pasha, but this would only have jarred on Oudney and Clapperton – and Denham was much less skilful in managing colleagues.

The first deep clashes of personality emerged early on the road to Fezzan in March 1822, reflecting differing attitudes to style and method of travel. The longer they travelled the more informal became the style adopted by the two naval men, setting them at variance with Denham's proclivity for formal and tight organisation. Trouble also began to brew over responsibility for navigation when it became clear that Denham lacked the skills of Clapperton, who was a trained and experienced hydrographic surveyor. When Denham gave his supposed subordinates instructions in writing about shared camp responsibilities, such as guard duties at night, they declined to respond or even comment.

It was by now becoming clear that the travellers were unable to work as a team. On both sides of the divide, they had stopped making any effort. Denham was writing home, to his brother Charles, about his dislike of the two Scotsmen, and of the insubordination of his 'assistant', Clapperton, describing Oudney as taciturn and obstinate, 'almost Dominie Sampson with more cunning', and Clapperton as overbearing and boastful, 'so vulgar, conceited and quarrelsome a person scarcely ever met with . . . this son of War, or rather Bluster'. Clapperton considered Denham incompetent to undertake any work of exploration since he 'could not read his sextant knew not a star in the sky and could not take the Altitude of the Sun'. Both sides complained, directly or indirectly, in their letters to Warrington, Barrow and the Colonial Office.

The first major crisis came, however, in the summer of 1822 in Murzuq. In late May, with no prospect of the Bey of Fezzan mounting an expedition across the Sahara for many months, nor apparently any other means of an escort being provided, Denham volunteered to return to Tripoli to remonstrate with Yusuf Pasha. Clapperton and Oudney took the opportunity of the enforced delay to travel in western Fezzan. On return to Murzuq in early August, Clapperton recorded:

> we found that a courier had arrived bringing us the intelligence that the Bashaw was not yet preparing to send an escort or army into the interior we found however that a kaffle was going to Bornou fourteen days after the Feast el Asser . . . and they would be glad of our company

They decided it was best to set off across the Sahara by themselves, while they could do so in the current dry season. This was a step they had had increasingly in mind since arrival in Murzuq. Safe travel through Fezzan and to Ghat had confirmed them in the belief that it was perfectly feasible to travel as a small, independent party with the help of Saharan merchants and local guides. As they now saw it, there was no need for, and indeed some disadvantage in, attachment to a large, armed escort.

On 6 September they were ready to leave, with a 'numerous and respectable caravan' of merchants which was on the point of departure, when they discovered to their great frustration that Abu Bakr Bu Khullum, a prosperous merchant and contender for the Beyship of Fezzan already well known to, and indeed like by, the Mission, had now been appointed to raise an escort. More infuriating was word from Warrington that Denham, after talks with Yusuf Pasha, had set off back to England. This they considered to be blatant dereliction of duty. In fact, Denham had decided to go home not just to complain in person to the Colonial Office about Karamanli's prevarications, but for reasons of personal ambition: to lobby for promotion in rank (confirmation of his majority and local rank of Lieutenant-Colonel, thus making him senior to Clapperton) and official endorsement of overall leadership of the expedition. From Marseilles he informed his brother he planned not to return to Tripoli until November.

Clapperton and Oudney were outraged and aired their frustration, anger and extremely frank criticism of Denham in a letter to Warrington. By this time, however, Denham had returned to Tripoli, having got no further than a spell of quarantine in Marseilles whence he was recalled by Warrington with the news of Bu Khulum's appointment. In Sockna in October, on his way back to Murzuq, Denham intercepted his companions' mail to the Consul General – as he was entitled to do, with 'letters in service to be considered public' – and was incensed in turn at the criticisms levelled at him. Denham's comment to his brother, that when he returned to join his companions he found morale in the Mission rather low, is hardly surprising.

In November Oudney, Denham and Clapperton at last set off southwards. Tyrwhitt, however, was recalled to Tripoli, Warrington's request that he remain in Murzuq as Vice-Consul having been turned down by the Colonial Office. The Mission travelled in two parties. Denham and his personal servants travelled with Bu Khulum; Oudney and Clapperton, with Hillman and the Mission's servant.

CUNNINGHAME GRAHAM IN THE ATLAS

Some comments and corrections on the reporting of this 1897 expedition

HAMISH BROWN

REREADING Alexander Maitland's biography of Robert and Gabriela Cunninghame Graham recently I rather choked over some of the descriptions of his Atlas escapade. They contain what might best be called geographical inexactitudes – not that we should be too hard on a book which is a good read and the author is generally as knowledgeable as the crowded Burtonesque footnotes indicate. The Atlas Mountains for C.G. (Cunninghame Graham) was a romantic adventure, tackled with gusto and dressed over all for launching on the public in 1898: *Magreb-el-Acksa: A Journey in Morocco.*

Just how vague the geographical knowledge was at the time can be seen in the map accompanying the book. The whole mountain part of the journey was on the Oued Nfis yet the river is not even shown, never mind it being wedged between parallel ranges and not opening an easy pass to the Suss. C.G. himself claimed to have followed the Nfis to its start, which is ridiculous, as is the claim that had they not been turned back, a short ride would have given them a distant view of Taroudant. A two day's ride at least would be truer and the city is not visible from the Tizi n' Test (tizi = pass) nor can one see Marrakech *and* Taroudant from any high point. (Sleeping on Jbel Toubkal I have been lucky to see the lights of Marrakech to the north and those of Ourzazate to the south from the 4167 summit, the highest spot in the Atlas and all North Africa). The Tsi-an-Test (*sic*) on C.G's map is actually shown *south* of the Oued Souss. The proportions of the map too are somewhat speculative.

On my wall I've a map of *c.*1850 which is even more vague. The Western Atlas is shown as being as extensive as everything eastwards to Jbel Ayachi, Miltsin (*sic*), south of Marocco (*sic*) is 'Highest Peak. Snow capped'. And M. Bibaouan (*sic*) is shown well to the northeast of

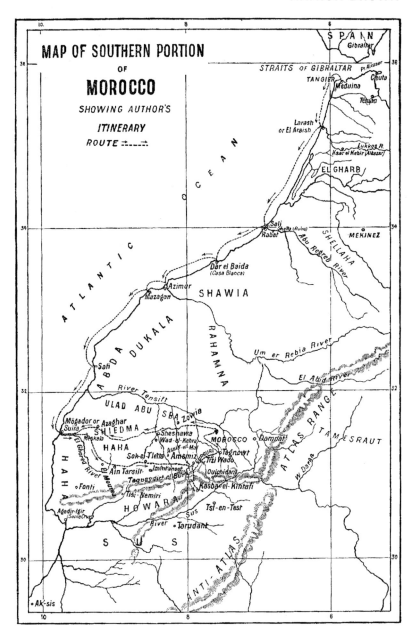

Map accompanying Magreb-el-Acksa *as published in 1898*

Taroudant. There's a delightful touch in showing Fighig (*sic*) with the comment 'said to be a large town'

The Bibaoun pass (Tizi Maachou) the easiest of the Triptich Tizis (Test, Tichka or its Telouet predecessor) was only made into a modern tarmac highway a quarter of a century ago, the now busy direct road from Marrakech to Agadir which debouches onto the Souss plain roughly half way between Agadir and Taroudant. Before that one either went over the Tizi n' Test (itself narrow and partly unsurfaced) or out to Essaouira and down the swooping coastal road which at times had bridges washed out by flash floods. There were no roads as such in 1897 when C.G. was in the Atlas.

C.G. travelled from Mogador (now Essaouira) to Imi-n-Tanout hoping to go through the 'easy' pass but as there was considerable blood letting he wended along the northern foothills of the Atlas towards Amizmiz to pick up the break in the chain where the Oued Nfis escapes the mountain fastness. The Oued Nfis actually rises in the Western Atlas up on the edge of the Tichka Plateau (*tichka* = high meadow) more or less north of Taroudant. It flows eastwards through gorges, forests and settlements for what would be several days' riding before turning north at modern Ourigane to escape onto the plains through a gorge, joins the Oued Tensift and reaches the Atlantic forty kilometres southwest of Safi. Ourigane does not appear in any map/records of a century ago; Tagadirt-n-Bour, a few kilometres up the Nfis being the name appearing instead.

There are enough names (both of then and now, however spelt) to make sense of C.G's travels. He mentions the Oued Nfis gorge and its drama. Leaving Tagadirt-n-Bour on the way back he climbed high onto the Kik Plateau east of the gorge and descended to the plains to reach Tamesloht, quite a day's ride, but C.G. was a famous horseman. Then as now the Koutoubia in Marrakech could be seen from afar off – and how much more thrilling when seen on a real journey, afoot or in the saddle, though I must say when the Marrakech train glides out from the Jbelet I peer excitedly to catch a first glimpse of the tower, the alluring logo of Marrakech and the snowy Atlas Mountains.

C.G. was rather glad to escape for the first snows had already fallen. All the early travellers mention snow on the Atlas – right back to Herodotus. Jackson and others noted snowy summits from Essaouira (I'm still hoping) and I wonder if Francis Drake saw snowy peaks when he

R. B. Cunninghame-Graham as Sheikh Mohammed El Fasi

gathered his ships off the coast here before committing to his round the world voyage.

C.G., coming in to the Nfis, noted salt deposits and heard of a mine; going out he looked down on salt pans from the climb to the plateau. Now a modern road allows the same view (still with salt works) as it corkscrews up, through and over to Amizmiz. He mentions cedars but I've not seen cedars anywhere in the Western Atlas. (Dorothy Dunnett in a thriller has cedars growing along the seafront at Essaouira!) The region is mostly forested with evergreen oak and some juniper. (Recent research shows some of Morocco's junipers are five thousand years old.)

From Taguaydirt-el-Bur (*sic*) C.G. rode on up the Nfis with considerably more difficulty than we face today. From a view point he mentions 'To the west towards the Sus the mountains seemed to dip, and Ouichidan, the highest peak in all the Southern Atlas, towered right above us a little to the east of where we stood, whilst far away in the dim distance rose the far distant mountains of the Anti-Atlas, which rise above the province of the Draa . . .' This is the sort of casual geography he is apt to produce. The Ouichidan crest (as he later shows) lies south of Talat-n-Yacoub where he would be detained and that was still a day's ride ahead to the SW! And from deep between ranges there is no way the Anti Atlas could be seen at all. And the Anti Atlas is hardly in the province of the Draa. Looking west from thereabouts one begins to have glimpses of Jbel Igdat, 3616m which is the highest summit west of the Toubkal block of peaks (climbed by Joseph Tomson in 1888.) The highest top on the Ouichidan crest is 3616m. The party spent the night at Imgordim which could be the current Imigdal.

They continued 'climbing staircases of rock, crossing and re-crossing the Wad el N'fis, passing deserted villages . . . A precipitous descent over red sandstone and through thickets of oleanders brought us where the bed of the N'fis spread out . . . The mountains, about ten miles away, formed a perfect semicircle, and Tisi Nemiri, upon our right, appeared to rise sheer from the river into the clouds.' On his right in fact is Jbel Gourza, 3280m, the first 3000'der to be climbed by outsiders, the Hooker, Ball, Maw party in 1871. Joseph Thomson also crossed this way, what he called the Tizi Nimiri to descend to the Goundafi *Kasbah*. There was no Tizi Nemiri to C.G's right and in a footnote he gives 'tisi = hill' which explains some misconceptions

Their guide declared the semi circle of peaks ahead to be 'the last ridge between us and the Sus, and with luck we ought to camp in the province of the Sus by evening'. That was considerable wishful thinking. At lunch time they were at the *Kasbah Goundafi* at Talat-n-Yacoub (C.G.'s Talet el Yacub) so in fact more than ten miles and 4000ft of ascent still lay ahead to reach the Tizi n' Test and a 7000ft descent to reach the Souss. Some afternoon's ride!

They talked their way past this caïdal fortress and 'After an hour of steep ascent over the shoulder of a mountain (*sic*) called Tisi m Test (Hill of the Oaks), we struck a steep staircase of rocks, and Mohammed said 'In an hour we shall pass a castle by the roadside, the guard house of the Caid, and from thence to the N'Zala is but half an hour . . . a few hours you will see the towers of Taroudant'. . ' They pushed on, and at the castle (Tagoundaft) an hour later, still believing to reach the Souss that day, they were caught up, arrested and taken back to the *Kasbah Goundafi* at Talat-n-Yacoub. And that was that. Creditable creativity however would turn the telling of the modest tale into a classic of Victorian derring do.

But the sloppy geography becomes even worse when biographers try and summarise at double remove. Maitland: 'Robert's journey ended . . . on 19 October with his capture by the Kaid of Kintafi *within a few miles of his goal* [my italics]'. Tschiffely in his biography invents: 'as they turned the sun broke through the clouds and Don Roberto had a glimpse of the tall towers and mosques of Tarudant'. They arrived at the Kasbah Goundafi in a deluge of rain to complete their misery.

He was detained for twelve days, initially camping in wet conditions and unprovided with food. He wrote to Tangier seeking consular help. ' . . . having been unable to cross to Sus by the Imintaunt we were obliged to take the road from Aurzuiz [Amizmiz] to Tizi which follows the river Nafees. All went well till within four hours of Tizi. At this point the Kaid arrested us.' Four hours from the pass/crest hardly tallies with the hope expressed in the book that they'd camp in the Souss that night.

C.G's description of the *kasbah* area is fine but though he has the Tizi Nimiri more correctly above him, he still believes it a mountain whereas it is a pass (on the map it is shown far northwest of Taroudant!) and another footnote gives an *azib* (goat shelter) as 'a country house or farm'. On the other side of the valley rises Ouichidan, 5000ft from the Nfis (it's actually a rise of less than 4000ft) and, annoyingly without being clear he comments 'a pass leads into Sus over a shoulder of the mountain. 'Is this mountain Ouichidan or Tizi n' Test (believing tizi = mountain)? I'd really like to know for from reading other sources I have a feeling there may be a muddle. There are two passes out to the Souss from the Nfis valley: the modern Tizi n' Test (which sounds like C.G's planned route as they were going on via the Kasbah Tagoundaft) or a pass over the Ouichidan crest which Joseph Thomson nearly reached when exploring up the Agoundis gorges while his companion was recovering at the Kasbah Goundafi from a scorpion bite received when changing into his pyjamas.

Joseph Thomson had come over the Tizi Nimiri (Tizi-n-Imiri on modern maps) and been horrified to find he was not looking down to the Souss but across to 'an opposing barrier of mountains called Wishdan [the pronunciation of Ouichidan] and, between, the great yawning glen of the Wad Nyfis, running parallel with the main axis. This cleft in the range was Gindafy . . . '

Hooker, Ball and Maw, climbed Jbel Gourza, just east of the Tizi-n-Imiri, calling it Jbel Tezza, which has led to speculations (was this a mistake for *tizi* or from Tizga, the name of a flanking village?) but I can verify their ascent beyond doubt as their description of summit buildings holds good (ruins today) and I've the identical picture of the peak as it appears in their book.

C.G. mentions his forerunners Hooker and Ball but not Joseph Thomson and I feel he could have been better prepared and so more accurate in his own descriptions. After all these sources were available. Even knowing the ground thoroughly myself I'm still left with some elements of puzzlement. I can note clearly where C.G. went but I'd dearly like the adventure to have continued to clarify the speculations of interest. The main *correction* I suppose is that he never escaped the Nfis Valley far less reaching anywhere near Taroudant. That was purpling the prose rather than geographical exactitude.

One person influenced by *Magreb-el-Acksa* was George Bernard Shaw who wrote the play *Captain Brassbound's Conversion* set in Mogador and a Caidal *kasbah* in the Atlas. The play is memorably forgettable but Conrad called Cunninghame Graham's book 'a glorious performance', and so it is.

C.G. visited Morocco many times before and after this visit, sometimes with his wife. The painters Crawhall and Lavery he knew in Tangier, and he travelled with Walter Harris several times, reaching Fes, Wazzan and the City of Morocco (Marrakech) again. Few people, after all, just visit Morocco once.

Titles mentioned

Cunninghame Graham, R. B., *Mogreb-el-Acksa*, 1898
Maitland, A, *Robert and Gabriela Cunninghame Graham*, 1983
Tschiffely, A. F., *47*
Don Roberto: Life and Works of R. B. Cunninghame Graham, 1937
Hooker, J. D. & Ball, J., *Journal of a Tour in Morocco and the Great Atlas*, 1878
Thomson, J., *Travels in the Atlas and Southern Morocco*, 1889

Other biographies

Watts, C. & Davies, L, *Cunninghame Graham: A Critical Biography*, 1979
West, H. F., A *Modern Conquistador*, R. B. Cunninghame Graham, 1932

Maps

The 1: 100,000 map sheets *Amezmiz* and *Tizi-n-Test* cover the area described while the Michelin map No. 959 *Morocco* has an enlarged inset which gives most of the vital names.

FOLLOW THE LEADER

Rosita Forbes and Hassanein Ahmed Bey and their journey through the Libyan desert to Kufara

BARNABY ROGERSON

T HE expedition to the Saharan oasis of Kufara in 1920-21 was one of the crowning achievements of Rosita Forbes. Nothing can rob of her that glory. However I believe her account of the expedition, the celebrated *The Secret of the Sahara: Kufara* does not give enough credit to the Egyptian explorer Hassanein Ahmed Bey. Rosita Forbes does not misplace a fact let alone a date, a name, or a compass reckoning, but uses a much more subtle literary technique – humour – to denigrate her companion and raise herself up as the leader of the expedition. She is not alone in this failing, indeed the whole long English tradition of travel-writing from pseudo-Mandeville to Kinglake's Eothen has always been wedded to making the reader laugh. About Rosita Forbes's abilities there can be no doubt.

Rosita Forbes is a one-off, a truly heroic traveller. Indeed she seems to come straight out of the pages of an interwar novel. She is like one of the side characters that fly in upon the plots of Evelyn Waugh or Scott Fitzgerald and leave behind a waft of unidentifiable scent and amoral glamour. The 1920s and 1930s were the days of her great travels, fame and achievement. She was in dash and bravour the female equivalent of Peter Fleming.

Rosita was born in 1893 in Lincolnshire into the fox-hunting county society and educated privately which allowed her to develop an obsession for maps and a desire to unlock the mystery of the unmapped world. A vivacious beauty, she married Colonel Ronald Forbes aged seventeen years old. She travelled through India, China and Australia with Colonel Forbes. Her reputation as a fast and wilful woman was completed when she left her husband after a few years of marriage and travelled back alone across Africa. She then drove an ambulance during the latter part of the First World war after which she travelled through the

Far East with a woman friend, pen-named Undine. These travels were described in her first book *Unconducted Wanderers*, published in 1919.

The following year saw her as a Paris based journalist with a strong leaning towards colonial affairs in Egypt and North Africa. This was a time of exceptional interest and she made the very most of her opportunities. On 28 November 1920 she arrived at the oasis of Jedabia, one hundred and ninety kilometres southwest of Benghazi in order to meet up with a well connected young Egyptian diplomat and explorer, Hassanein Ahmed Bey. Together they would travel south across the Libyan desert by camel to visit Kufara, the distant and reclusive Saharan oasis, that had once served as the headquarters of the Senussi. The Senussi were a Muslim brotherhood devoted to returning Islam back to its true early form, in today's parlance they were fundamentalists. It was an extraordinary physical achievement, the journey completed when they rode their camels back into the Egyptian oasis of Siwa on 19 February 1921. The only account of it we have is that by Rosita Forbes.

The Secret of the Sahara: Kufara was well received and sold well. First published in 1921 it received even wider circulation in 1937 as one of the early Penguin Books (no 113) in the magenta livery given to Travel & Adventure paperbacks. It is very good account, detailed enough to bring the characters and the landscape alive, filled with historical insights, maps and sense of adventure, mystery, achievement and humour.

My first reading was entirely uncritical. My eyes were only gradually opened to its possible inaccuracies when I began to investigate the career of the Egyptian diplomat and Saharan explorer, Hassanein Ahmed Bey. Within a closed circle I learned that he was widely admired for staying silent about the book, though his friends, colleagues and family considered the book a travesty. Even the National Dictionary of Biography's entry on Rosita Forbes (normally not the most hostile of critics) records the upset her Kufara book caused in Egypt. In their eyes, the non-Muslim, non-Arabic speaking British female journalist was just a passenger. It was Hassanein Ahmed Bey who was the resourceful director and mastermind of the expedition. I was told that the reason that Rosita Forbes had reversed the roles in her book was in revenge for slighted love. It seems a characteristically Egyptian explanation but not out of place for in their different ways both Rosita and Hassanein earned scandalous 'reputations'. According to this account Rosita had been in

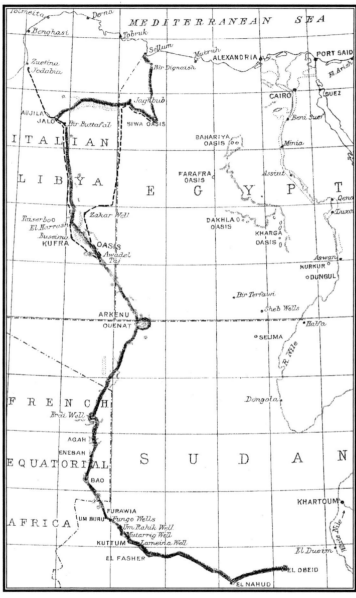

Route of Rosita Forbes and Hassanein Bey in 1921 – – – – – – –

Route of Hassanein Bey in 1923

| 0 | 100 | 200 | 300 | 400 | 500 | miles |

| 0 | 100 | 200 | 300 | 400 | 500 | kilometres |

love with Hassanein, that they may have had an affair, but that he couldn't marry her and so she put her revenge in the pages of the book. Indeed this may explain a slightly mysterious paragraph in Rennell Rodd's Introduction to Hassanein's own book, *The Lost Oases*, 1925. Here Rodd wrote, 'He has occasionally consulted me as an elder friend . . . on certain matters of personal interests to himself. I may therefore claim to know him intimately and I cannot refrain from recording my testimony that in all such questions, and especially in a very delicate matter which he submitted to me, I have always found him generous in his judgements and, for I know no other way of expressing what I mean, a great gentleman.' I feel that this (admittedly opaque half-paragraph) refers to the honourable silence Hassanein maintained over Mrs Rosita Forbes descriptions of him. It also seem to gently support the rumours of some love affair between the two of them. However whatever the emotional reality I know enough about travel-writers to know that love or no love they also have a strong tendency to airbrush out other characters and place themselves in the centre of the stage. Indeed there is at least one famous, alive and productive travel-writer who makes all his travelling companions sign a contract of literary silence so as to guarantee that his account remains uncontradicted.

We will return to the text of Kufara later but let us first continue with Rosita Forbes's career as a travel-writer. She got married for a second time in 1921, produced a novel set in the Near East, *The Jewel in the Lotus* before continuing her exploration of Arabia and North Africa. *El Raisuni: Sultan of the Mountains* – a biography of the Moroccan bandit-governor of the western Rif that was published in 1924. This was followed by a one-thousand-mile journey through Abyssinia capped by the book and film *Red Sea to Blue Nile*, in 1925. A tour of the Balkans dominated 1928, her journey through Central Asia most of 1929 and 1930. The next book, *Conflict* in 1931 was about the Middle East. *Eight Republics in Search of a Future* – published in 1933 chronicles her long travel through South America two years before. *Forbidden Road: Kabul to Samarkand* published in 1937 covers her Central Asians travels followed by her Raj book *India of the Princes* published in 1939.

Real People (1937) and *These Men I Knew* (1940) and *Appointment in the Sun* (1949) concludes her impressive list of works. These last three books are halfway to being memoirs but include a number of good

*Hassanein Ahmed Bey and
Rosita Forbes*

adventures from her journalistic assignments for the *Daily Telegraph* and *Sunday Times* as well as meetings with such leading men of the day as Hitler, Abdel Krim of the Rif rebellion, Ibn Saud – the founder of Saudi Arabia and Kemal Ataturk – the founder of modern Turkey. Indeed it is almost easier to make a list of the autocrats of the 1930s she did not meet.

Her interest in the power and the charisma of rulers had led her on some extraordinary quests and privileged interviews but also led her dangerously close to an admiration of the fascist strongmen of that era. It was rumoured that she had a passing affair with Mussolini and certainly interviewed Hitler a number of times. By 1940 her reputation was diminished if not finished and she would end her life as an expatriate exile in the Bahamas where she died in the late 1960s.

Now almost totally neglected she will no doubt one day be revived and recognised as one of the great British women travel-writers to be put on the pantheon alongside Isabella Bird, Freya Stark, Lesley Blanch and Marianne North.

Having saluted her personal achievement it is time to look at six examples from the text of *The Secret of The Sahara: Kufara*.

In each of these Rosita Forbes cuts Hassanein Bey down from being the leader of the expedition to an endearing but childish figure, in her own words a useful ally. Firstly from the Preface, ' I have dedicated the story of our adventures to my co-explorer Ahmed Bey Hassanein, for his knowledge of the Senussi acquired during his secretaryship to the Talbot Mission in 1916 was invaluable to me, and he was the loyalest of my allies throughout the expedition..' Notice that despite Rosita's praise Hassanein is merely 'invaluable to me' and the 'loyalest of my allies', hardly appropriate for the leader and organiser of an expedition.

On page 16 of the Penguin edition she writes, 'his knowledge of the language, religion and customs was invaluable to me, Hassanein Bey assured me that he came for a rest cure. Later on he assumed so many characters that it was somewhat difficult to keep count. He was always the Q.M.G. of our little expedition and he used to produce macaroons at the most impossible moments from equally impossible places! He was a chaperon when elderly sheikhs demanded my hand in marriage, a fanatic of the most bitter type when it was necessary to impress the local mind, my Imam when we prayed in public, a child when he lost his only pair of primrose yellow slippers, a cook when we stole a bottle of Marsala from the last Italian fort . . . ' Again this amusing peon of praise helps Rosita place Hassanein less as a leader than as an ideal travelling companion doubling as an occasional butler . . .

This image is further belittled by the first of her 'packing' stories, which for all their possible venom I still find ticklishly amusing. From page 17 of the Penguin edition, 'However, on the day of our departure from Benghazi he was distinctly subdued, for, on looking at our piles of camp kit and my two very small suitcases, I had suddenly noticed several large and heavy leather bags. With horror I demanded if they were all absolutely necessary to his personal comfort. 'Yes, really!' he assured me. 'They are only actual necessities. As a matter of fact they are half empty. I thought they would be useful for putting things in.' The words were hardly out of his mouth when one of the opulent-looking cases, slipping from the Arab servant's hand, burst open and deposited at my feet a large bottle of 'Heure bleue' bath salts, several packets of salted almonds and a sticky mass of chocolates and marrons glacés, together with a pair of patent leather shoes and a resplendent Balliol blazer. Words failed me! 'Necessities!' I stuttered as I marched towards the camion to see that the heaviest cases were not put on top of the large rather fragile fanatis for carrying water.' Here Rosita reduces Hassanein to some foppish thing out of from the pages of P. G. Wodehouse while she comes over as the serious one.

This is repeated on page 26, 'The most amusing part of the business was afforded by the spies who constantly surrounded us and who were so thrilled with their own importance that I used to have daily fights with Hassanein Bey to prevent him playing delightful little comedies to excite them still more.'

Worse is to follow when she describes Hassanein falling upon the gifts of the Senussi (from page 28), 'There was also a tarboush and a pair of wonderful yellow slippers. Before the faltering words were out of my mouth, Hassanein Bey had pounced upon the yellow slippers. His expression was that of a small child when a much-loved doll has been restored to it. "Hamdulillah!" he exclaimed, and fled, clutching his prize.' Nothing else in the book quite equals this description for its belittling power. Though there are numerous other 'packing scenes' such as that on page 36 which reveal 'seven different coloured bottles of eau de Cologne and a mass of heterogeneous attire more suited to Bond Street than the Sahara. I had to superintend the packing lest he ignore the claims of malted milk tablets, towels and woollen underclothing in favour of delicately striped shirts and a lavender silk dressing-gown!' Repeated again on page 43, 44 and 45. The gender roles are perfectly swopped when she describes herself shouting, "You have exactly six minutes in which to get ready," I said in an awful voice. A chair fell with a crash, breaking an eau de Cologne bottle and sending a mass of little tubes, bottles and boxes rolling to my feet. . . . He submitted to being pushed and pulled into the white garments he had to wear . . . I believe I banged a white *kufiya* on his head and flung an agal at him before rushing from the room to take up my position behind the main door . . . '

These quotations are of course taken out of context and can be balanced by an equal number of more dispassionate descriptions. However there is no escaping their accumulative effect which is to diminish Hassanein and raise up the status of Rosita Forbes as director of the expedition.

Hassanein Bey was too much of a gentleman of the old school of manners to publicly criticise Rosita Forbes let alone take her to the law court. Even in his own book, *The Lost Oasis*, which was published just a few years later he describes his own much more extensive Saharan exploration but does not air one word of criticism.

Hassanein was at least as extraordinary and as exceptional figure as Rosita. He is the very definition of a Muslim Arab British-Egyptian gentleman. The son of the Sheikh of the Al-Azahar mosque (the Egyptian equivalent of the Archbishop of Canterbury) and grandson of the Admiral in Chief of the Egyptian navy. His connections at court were impeccable and he had been hand picked by King Fouad to finish his education at Balliol College at the English University of Oxford which he represented for fencing. On his return to Egypt he worked for the Ministry of the Interior at Cairo and during a period of British enforced martial law was attached to the staff of General Sir John Maxwell. During the First World War he was a key player in the Anglo-Egyptian strategy that turned the Senussi brotherhood from a relentless enemy to a sworn friend. At the start of the war the reigning Senussi pursued a pro-Turkish and pan-Islamic policy of attacking the British army in Egypt supported by arms and advice from Germany and Turkey. Half way through the war the Senussi brotherhood realised that they had backed the wrong horse, and the pro-British (or should one say pro Anglo-Egyptian) cousin took over.

Hassanein Bey was in the 1917 mission, led by Colonel Milo Talbot that patched up a dignified peace with this new leader, Sayed Idris El Senussi. He had already made personal contact with Sayed Idris two years before at Mecca during the Haj. It was only this vital contact that allowed the 1920 Kufara expedition to take place, for Hassanein Bey would travel as the guest of the Senussi through their desert and stay in their oases. Originally he planned to travel with his old Balliol friend, Francis Rodd. Rodd was also part of the Saharan scene, to the extent that his father Sir Rennel Rodd was one of the greatest British explorers of the central Sahara and whose book about the Tuareg, *People of the Veil*, remains a definitive work. Indeed as we have already seen Sir Rennel would later write an introduction to Hassanein's *The Lost Oasis*. It was Francis Rodd who had asked if Rosita Forbes could join the expedition and then at the last moment was unable to come himself. Viewed from this light it can be quite clearly seen that right from the start it was Hassanein Bey's expedition and Hassanein Bey's expertise. He also had a strong personal motive for the expedition which can be seen as an extension of his diplomatic and political career. Rosita Forbes, far from being the leader, came along as a friend of a friend.

For his great Saharan expedition which set off in December 1922 (for which he was later awarded the Founder's Medal by the Royal Geographical Society) Hassanein Bey decided to travel without any guest companions. There must have been strong memories of his previous experience. These memories might have informed his introductory chapter in which he compares the desert with a woman. 'It is though a man were deeply in love with a very fascinating but cruel woman. She treats him badly, and the world crumples in his hand; at night she smiles on him and the whole world is a paradise.'

Hassanein Bey later rose through the government ranks to become Royal Chamberlain to the young King Farouk and the chief advisor to the Dowager Queen. He was one of the key figures in Egyptian politics and society throughout the 1930s and 1940s. He was married to Yussfry the daughter of Saifullah Yussfry, a fellow diplomat of Hassanein's during his term of duty in the USA. His mother-in-law was the redoutable Princess Chevekhiar, one of the grandest and richest of Egyptian high society (whose town house was large enough to be taken over as the home of the National Assembly). The Chevekhiar's were also descended from the royal house of Mohammed Ali. Hassanein was wedged into the very centre of Egyptian society and was one of the cornerstones of Anglo-Egyptian accord. Indeed when the young King Farouk was on the point of being forced off his throne by a British military 'palace coup' Lord Lambton records that it was a whisper from Hassanein into the King's ear that defused the situation. He is described as 'full of pleasantness, conviviality, very charming, yet all seeing and totally observant. He revealed nothing and was totally impenetrable.' He died at the height of his powers in 1947 when his car was hit by an army lorry on one of the Cairo bridges over the Nile.

THE SLAVE TRADE ROUTES OF THE CENTRAL SAHARA

JOHN WRIGHT

THE SAHARA is a formidable natural harrier, but not an impassable one. The world's largest hot desert is believed to have changed little in form or climate over the past four thousand years. Traders have certainly been crossing it, from the Mediterranean coastlands in the north to the inner African bush country in the south, for at least the last three thousand years. This has always been a hazardous undertaking, not least because the Sahara is so vast: about the size of the continental United States. To cross the desert, even at its easiest and narrowest point, between Tripoli and Lake Chad, is almost the equal of a journey from Tripoli to London – that is, in terms of distance, not difficulty or danger.

Southbound trading caravans normally carried the produce and manufactures of the Mediterranean world to exchange for the raw materials of inner Africa: black slaves, gold and any other available and marketable goods that could withstand the high costs and high risks of desert transport. This was a trade in goods which, whatever their initial prices, were costly luxuries when once delivered to final buyers on the far side of the Sahara.

The trans-Saharan trade routes ended at suitable northern oasis-markets, or at the very few safe harbours on North Africa's exposed and surprisingly inhospitable Mediterranean coast. On the far side of the desert they reached the great entrepot-markets of Black Africa, the collecting centres for the raw produce of the inner continent.

Such roads were not even tracks in any recognised sense, but rather

---

1   J. Bruce Lockhart and J. Wright (eds), *Difficult and Dangerous Roads: Hugh Clapperton's Travels in Sahara and Sudan, 1822–1825*, (London, 2000), Introduction, pp. 3–4

a general line of travel between two points.[2] They had been tried and proven by many generations of travellers for their accessibility, their relative security, and the services and amenities offered at oases and resting places along the line of march. But vital above all to any route were regular water sources able to slake the urgent thirsts of an arriving caravan of hundreds of humans and animals.[3] Clearly, the Saharan environment offered few such roads, particularly for slow merchant caravans encumbered by gangs of exhausted trade slaves.

In the eastern Sahara the River Nile – despite its cataracts – was one approach from northern to inner Africa, while the celebrated *Darb al'Arbain* (Forty Days' Road) from Asiut in upper Egypt to Kordofan, was a more direct, if more hazardous, choice by land. In the western Sahara, well-used desert roads led from such Moroccan entrepots as Sijilmasa and later Marrakesh to the gold-markets of Ancient Ghana and Mali, and also to the rich trading milieu-of the Niger Bend. Similarly, Algiers, Constantine and Tunis all had their own trans-Saharan trade links through Ouargla and the Tuat oases to the Hausa states and the middle Niger.[4]

Different Saharan roads predominated at different times. But since the early Islamic era, the main traffic tended to shift from the western routes to the central roads and finally, in the nineteenth and early twentieth centuries, to the most easterly, from Benghazi to Wadai.[5] Yet the least important of the Barbary capitals, Tripoli, has always drawn traffic to its three direct trans-Saharan roads to inner Africa. The map (p. 58) explains whys Tripoli lies further south than any other Maghrebi Mediterranean port and is closer to the Sahara itself and thus to the Sudan, the lands of the black peoples beyond the Great Desert.[6]

One of these roads from Tripoli exploited the phenomenon of the small and isolated oasis of Ghadames, with its own links southwestwards

2   J. Chapelle, *Nomades noirs du Sahara: les Toubous*, (Paris, 1982), p. 31

3   L. C. Briggs, *Tribes of the Sahara*, (Cambridge, Mass., 1960), pp. 9, 28–30

4   see Bruce Lockhart and Wright, *Difficult and Dangerous Roads*, Map 1, 'Trade Routes of the Sahara in the early Nineteenth Century'; see also n. 15, p. 5

5   J. Wright, 'The Wadai–Benghazi Slave Route' in E. Savage (ed.), *The Human Commodity: Perspectives on the Trans Saharan Slave Trade*, (London, 1992). p. 174

6   *Bilad al-Sudan* (Arabic), the Land of the Blacks, all the band of country south of the Sahara and north of the tropical forest belt

to the rich sub-Saharan markets of the Hausa States and, beyond them, the Niger Bend. Tripoli's two other roads took advantage of the natural corridor of the Fezzanese oases, about one-third of the way between the Tripolitanian coast and the southern edge of the central desert at Lake Chad. They also lie about midway between the Niger Bend to the southwest and Egypt to the northeast, allowing one of the Sahara's very few diagonal, as opposed to north-south roads. The Fezzanese oases were thus the essential halting places on the long cross-desert journeys between 'white' North Africa and the "black" inner continent.

Tripoli is the sole survivor of the trio of trading stations founded within less than two hundred miles of each other on the difficult Tripolitanian coast by the merchant Phoenicians some two thousand five hundred years ago. Tripoli has never been a particularly rich town, at least not compared with other North African trading cities; but it seems also to have survived because of its advantageous position on the central Mediterranean narrows, providing fair sailing to Malta, Sicily, Italy and, via Crete, to the eastern Mediterranean. But, above all, the survival of Tripoli and its Saharan trade routes over many centuries right to the beginning of the twentieth was due to their role as main arteries and outlets of the cross-desert trade in black slaves. These were marched across the desert in surprisingly consistent numbers as part of regular yearly caravans meeting the incessant, indeed insatiable, demands of North African, Mediterranean and Middle Eastern Islam for black servant girls and concubines.[7] The trans-Saharan trades in other raw African products, including the gold trade that dominated the western roads at least up to the late middle ages, were never as consistent, or as regular, as what Oric Bates characterised as "the thin but unending stream of slaves".[8]

These slaves reached Tripoli by two of the three available main roads. Most came by the ancient track, good but dreary, named the Garamantian road after the ancient Garamantes people of Fezzan mentioned by Herodotus.[9] It ran more or less due north across the desert from

7   W. D. Phillips, *Slavery from Roman Times to the Earls Transatlantic Trade*, (Manchester, 1985), pp. 73–4; M. Gordon, *Slavery in the Arab World*, (New York, 1989), pp. 79–104

8   O. Bates, *The Eastern Libyans An Essay*, (London, 1914), pp. 102–3

9   Herodotus, *The Histories* (trans. De Selincourt, Harmondsworth, 1954), Book IV, 123, pp. 303–4

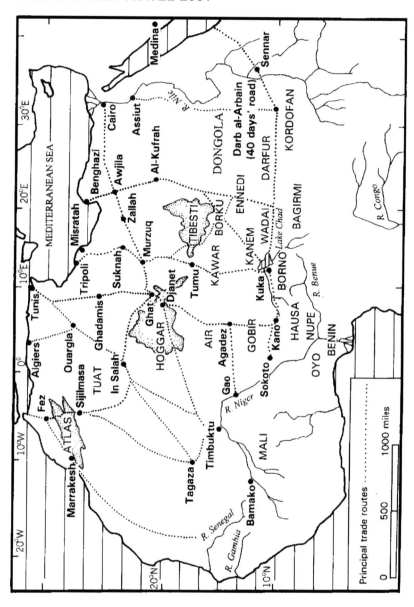

Lake Chad, After leaving the relatively easy travelling conditions of the Chadian *sahel*,[10] it passed up the corridor of the Kawar oasis-chain, crossing the foothills of the Tibesti and Hoggar massifs by the wells of Tummo and Bir Meshru. It then skirted the Murzuk Sand Sea to the east, to reach the current main slaving entrepot of Fezzan, for different oases predominated at different times. Murzuk did so from the sixteenth century onwards. From Fezzan, the road continued by fairly easy stages – easy, that is, by Saharan standards – across the Gebel Soda and through the Giofra oases to the Mediterranean at Misurata, and so along the coast to Tripoli. The total distance covered is over twelve hundred miles, or some sixty days of actual travelling at an average of twenty miles per day, but excluding the longer halts.

All but the most valuable slaves made that journey on foot, sometimes carrying loads of up to twenty pounds on their heads. Even the little children too big for their mothers to carry put in their twenty daily miles. As the mid-nineteenth century British Saharan traveller, James Richardson, remarked, 'Most of those poor wretches had performed journeys on their way to bondage which would invest me with imperishable renown as a traveller should I accomplish them.'[11]

This Garamantian road was very likely one of the world's oldest trading routes: it has certainly been in use for at least two and half thousand years. It offered the comparatively easy, well-watered and secure travelling that usually ensured the safe passage of large, slow and straggling slave caravans with no more than an acceptable ten per cent loss of slave lives – that is, unless disaster struck, as it did in August 1849 when all sixteen hundred slaves in one Tripoli-bound caravan died of thirst when a well failed.[12] None but the smallest slave caravans used the second available road from Fezzan to Tripoli. This followed the more direct but far harder route across the sterile, stony Plateau of the Hammada al-Hamra and through Mizda: it was a road for travellers in a hurry.

10 *sahel* (Arabic), shore: the wide northern and southern pre-desert fringes of the Sahara

11 J. Richardson, *Narrative of a Mission to Central Africa 1850–51*, (2 Vols., London, 1853), Vol I, p. 23

12 Public Record Office, Kew, London, Foreign Office Papers: FOI60/12, Gagliuffi [Vice Consul, Tripoli] to John D. Reade, 14 September 1849

The other main slaving road to Tripoli, passing through the small, isolated oasis of Ghadames, was longer and harder than the Fezzan road. Ghadamsi merchants dealt in slaves and other merchandise traded through the Niger Bend countries, and particularly through the Hausa States. To trek from the Niger to the Mediterranean at Tripoli, slaves passed northwards through the Tuat oases and then northeast to Ghadames. Another slaving road led from Gao on the Niger to Agades in Air, where it met the main northbound road from Hausaland. The next stage was due northwards to Ghat, with its direct access either to Ghadames or to Murzuk. Ghadames, the Saharan entrepot for both Tripoli and Tunis, was thus served by two main desert routes, offering alternative means of supply in the likely event of troubles somewhere or other along the way.

The few reliable Saharan slave trade statistics available before the mid-nineteenth century suggest that Murzuk was in most years a more important slave entrepot than Ghadames.[13] Murzuk always had the advantage of more sources of supply than Ghadames. Its traders could buy slaves from a very wide swathe of inner Africa to make up caravans crossing the desert by the Garamantian road; they could also draw slaves from the southwest through Ghat; and they did occasionally deal in blacks brought up by a feasible if roundabout route from the Sultanate of Wadai, far to the southeast. Murzuk traders had the further advantage of Mediterranean slave outlets which, at least until the 1850s, were largely immune to the European abolitionist pressures that had by then almost ruined the trade through Tunis and French Algeria. Thus from Murzuk slaves could be taken either to Tripoli, or the nearer Mediterranean port at Misurata, or northeastwards to Augila oasis. That was the junction of tracks leading either to the part of Benghazi, or to Siwa oasis in the Western Desert, on the road to the teeming slave markets of Cairo. For much of the nineteenth century, the Ottoman Turkish authorities at Tripoli, Misurata, Benghazi, Derna and the smaller Mediterranean outlets positively encouraged the black slave traffic as the sole fairly reliable source of revenue from an otherwise largely destitute economy.[14]

---

13 J. Wright, *'Nothing Else but Slaves': Britain and the Central Saharan Slave Trade in the Mid-Nineteenth Century*, unpublished Ph.D. thesis, London, 1998. Table 2.2, 'Slave Arrivals in Tripoli, 1753–56', Table 7.1, 'Slaves Arriving in Murzuk from 1843 to 1854'; Table 8.1, 'The Slave Trade through Ghadames'

14 J. Wright, *'Nothing Else but Slaves'*, op. cit., p. xxx

In the early nineteenth century a new and important slave road – probably the most difficult of all those across the Sahara – was opened through the eastern desert by a rising slaving power, the Sultanate of Wadai.[15] It crossed the high plateau of Borku (where the frigid winter nights killed the naked trade slaves in droves) and followed long waterless stretches on either side of the secluded oases of Kufra. From Kufra, slaves trekked to Augila for onward movement to Benghazi, or across the Western Desert to Egypt. The Wadai road remained a leading slave outlet for longer than any others despite the French occupation of Wadai in 1909 and the Italian seizure of Benghazi and other Cyrenaican ports in 1911, caravans continued to use the road's middle sections up to the Italian occupation of Kufra in 1931.[16]

Such were the outlines of the Saharan trading network of the nineteenth century. But these tracks were the highways of a complex trading system that not only linked the two sides of the Sahara, but also served the many settled and nomadic communities of the desert. As Ross E. Dunn has pointed out:

> No desert oasis, however lonely and unimportant, was isolated from the lines of trade. To describe the commercial system . . . in terms of particular routes and specialising groups is certainly to oversimplify it, for caravans, large and small, went everywhere that people lived. Traders carried not only merchandise, but also news, ideas and opinions.[17]

Moreover, the patterns of Saharan trade, as they existed about 1850, were not fixed or static. Merchants and market traders, although hopelessly conservative in many ways, were able to act with surprising initiative and speed to pressures and changes in the desert itself, or from both sides of it. They could switch routes, markets and outlets to avoid such perceived threats to their business as tribal insecurity, punitive Turkish taxation, or European abolitionist fervour, or to take advantage of

---

15 D. D. Cordell, 'Eastern Libya, Wadai and the Sanusiya: a Tariqa and a Trade Route', *Journal of African History*, XVIII, 1 (1977), pp. 21–36.

16 R. Forbes, *The Secret of the Sahara: Kufara*, (London, 1921), p. 109; A. M. Hassanein Bey, *The Lost Oases*, (London, 1925), p. 179; K. Holmboe, *Desert Encounter: An Adventurous Journey through Italian Africa*, (London, 1936), p. 188.

17 R. B. Dunn, *Resistance in the Desert: Moroccan Responses to French Imperialism, 1881–1912*, (London, 1977), p. 130.

new trading opportunities. Thus the oasis of Ghat – in effect a free-trade zone well beyond the reaches of Turkish bureaucracy – rose to new prosperity and prominence in mid-century as the trade first through Ghadames and then through Murzuk became increasingly difficult. Similarly, the Wadai–Benghazi road undoubtedly gained from worsening mid-century conditions on the more westerly routes. Very likely, the patterns of Saharan trade had also evolved and shifted in earlier centuries in response to internal and external factors, but little is known of such changes. Although even the nineteenth century evidence is scanty, it is nevertheless clear that conditions were by then especially difficult, with the ancient desert trade all but collapsing at the century's end. This was due, first, to European abolitionist pressure on the slave trade that was the mainstay of the whole antiquated and unreformed system that could not keep going merely on the meagre profits of 'legitimate' trade in ivory, skins and exotic plant products. For the system itself was unable to adapt to the economic, financial, political and other globalising tendencies of the late nineteenth century; it was eventually overwhelmed by European economic and colonial pressures.[18]

The origins of the Saharan trade in black slaves are unknown. But it is certain that traffic across the central desert, at least, became highly important soon after the Islamic conquest of North Africa in the seventh century, with black women and girls in particular demand for service in Islamic households. This is why, at least according to British consular statistics of the nineteenth century, about two-thirds of all slaves taken across the Sahara were females. The processes of raiding, enslaving, selection, sale and resale of trade slaves were usually long and complex, with the high death-rate through mistreatment and neglect merely reflecting the sheer abundance and cheapness of supplies. Very few indeed of those originally raided as slaves deep in the African interior by fellow-Africans were eventually exported into and across the Sahara.

It is not easy to estimate the size of this trade, since reliable figures are lacking for all but a few years in the mid-nineteenth century, and these do not tell the whole story.[19] But, according to recent calculations, between AD600 and 1900, about fourteen million slaves may have crossed

18 J. Wright, 'Nothing Else but Slaves', op. cit., p. xxx
19 Ibid., p. 10

the Sahara, with the trade reaching and continuing at an average rate of twenty thousand a year from 1400 onwards.[20] These figures by the French geographer–historian Raymond Mauny are seriously questioned by Ralph Austen, who suggests that over the same period less than ten million slaves may have started the crossing, with less than seven and a half million of those reaching Mediterranean North Africa. This was because Austen estimates that five per cent were sold to desert communities, while twenty per cent died on the road.[21] The Saharan slave trade never matched the scale or scope of the Atlantic trade's peak years of the eighteenth and early nineteenth centuries. But the fact that it quietly persisted for nearly ten times longer than the Atlantic traffic did, suggest that the total number of black Africans consumed by the two separate systems may have been roughly equal: perhaps twenty million slaves altogether.

Responding to the new enthusiasm for statistics, the British government decided that it needed to know more about the size and the workings of the central Saharan slave trade. Such knowledge was needed before suitable pressure was put on the Ottoman Turkish government to abolish the traffic once and for all. A British vice consulate was accordingly opened at Murzuk in 1843, the main market of the central desert; another was opened at Ghadames in 1850. For a few years, both posts provided annual statistics of slave traffic through these places; see table 1, below.

At the same time, the British consulate general in Tripoli and the vice consulates at Benghazi, Derna and, in 1854 and 1855 only, at Misurata began to send the Foreign Office returns of slave shipments from these ports on the Mediterranean 'middle passage'. Among the many destinations were slave markets in Ottoman Crete, the Aegean islands, northern Greece (especially Turkish Salonica), Albania and Anatolia, as well as Smyrna and Constantinople itself. Thus for some twelve years, from 1843–54, there are fairly reliable and consistent runs of slave trade figures which make it possible to 'reconstruct' the main features of the central Saharan traffic at that time.

Yet these British figures by no means tell the whole story. They are not complete for every year, while much of the traffic, particularly by

20 R. Mauny, *Les siècles obscurs de l'Afrique noire*, (Paris, 1971), pp. 240–1
21 R. A. Austen, 'The Mediterranean Islamic Slave Trade out of Africa: A Tentative Census', in Savage, *The Human Commodity*, pp. 214–48.

Table 1 – The Slave Trade through Murzuk and Ghadames 1843–54

	Murzuk	Ghadames
1843	2000	
1844	1509	
1845	1105	
1846	1075	
1847	1281	
1848	1257	389
1849	1550	429 (estimate)
1850	2000 (estimate)	400 (estimate)
1851	2200 (estimate)	226
1852	2458	600 (estimate)
1853	2609	518
1854	2900	557

Sources: Public Record Office, Kew, London: Foreign Office Papers, FO 84 (Slave Trade) for relevant years

smaller caravans using the lesser tracks, simply escaped official British notice. So did the private sales in closed houses of the more costly slaves, including eunuchs and girls of exceptional beauty or skills. And slavers, anxious to avoid often arbitrary Turkish taxes, and wary of the abolitionist fervour of European officials, were at best reluctant informants.

Nevertheless, the British vice consul, Giambattista Gagliuffi at Murzuk kept fairly full yearly returns of slaves arriving there. These show that from 1843 to 1849, the average yearly import was just under fourteen hundred slaves. These people came from an extraordinarily wide extent of inner Africa: in modern terms, they were drawn from as far off as the western Sudan Republic (Darfur) and the middle of Nigeria (Nupe), and from all the lands in between. But Gagliuffi gave Murzuk's main source of supply – about three-quarters of the total – as 'Bornu'. This did not necessarily mean that the Empire of Bornu was the slaves' homeland. For most were originally from remoter parts of inner tropical Africa. Such slaves were marshalled at the great slave market of Bornu at Kuka (Kukawa), just west of Lake Chad, where seemingly almost arbitrary market processes selected a small proportion of those on sale for the Saharan trade, the rest finding ready local buyers. The second source of slaves for the Murzuk market, again according to vice consul Gagliuffi, was 'Sudan', or Hausaland. Like Bornu, the Hausa states had their depots where some slaves of many different origins were destined for the Sahara crossing. Slaves do not seem to have been selected in any way for their fitness to make such a journey: those who failed to keep up with the caravan were eventually abandoned in the desert.[22] Slaves from the Hausa states reached Fezzan by travelling first to Bornu and then crossing the desert from Lake Chad by the same ancient Garamantian road that the slave caravans from Bornu itself took.

Although the road from Lake Chad delivered about eighty-five per cent of all slave imports into Murzuk in the 1840s, some slaves were also sent up every year from Hausaland to Murzuk through Air and Ghat. The length and harshness of this road can be read in the irregularity with which slave caravans used it: in some years, over two hundred slaves arrived by this route, in others only twenty or so. Very occasionally, slaves also reached Murzuk from Wadai by a route so long and exhausting that it is hard to imagine how any of them survived the journey.

Slave traffic through Murzuk more or less doubled in the early 1850s, compared with ten years earlier. This greater activity may have been due to merchants' fears of impending Turkish abolition, or changes in the Turkish tax regime in Fezzan, or greater security on the Bornu road, or a combination of all three factors. In 1852 Murzuk imported just under 2,500 slaves, over 2,600 in 1853 and nearly 3,000 in 1854. These seem to have been exceptional years. After 1854 there are no more reliable figures because vice consul Gagliuffi then stopped reporting, his successors made no slave trade returns at all, and the Murzuk post was closed in 1861.[23]

The trade through Ghadames was far smaller. The French consul in Tripoli had reported in the mid-eighteenth century that between four hundred and six hundred slaves a year were passing through that oasis-market. A century later, according to British consular statistics for 1848–54, the traffic was still about the same. But Ghat was by then

22 Eye witness accounts of this fate are provided by such British Saharan travellers as George Lyon (*A Narrative of Travels in Northern Africa in the Years 1818, 1819 and 1820*, London, 1821), p. 329 and Hugh Clappertonn (Bruce Lockhart and Wright, *Difficult and Dangerous Roads*, pp. 215, 275).

23 A. A. Boahen, *Britain: the Sahara and the Western Sudan, 1788–1861*, (Oxford, 1964), pp. 213–34.

becoming more important, apparently dealing in about a thousand slaves a year for the markets of southern Algeria and Tunisia, Murzuk, Ghadames and Trivoli.[24] And over to the east, the new road from Wadai to Benghazi was by 1850 handling up to two thousand slaves a year for the Cyrenaic, Egyptian and East Mediterranean markets.[25]

Even by contemporary standards, this was not a rich trade. The common and mostly young trade slaves taken along these central Saharan roads for sale and resale in the public markets were not worth all that much.

Table 2 – Slave Prices in US$s per head, 1851		
	Young male *(with beard beginning)*	Young female *(with breasts plump)*
Kano	$8–12	$32
Murzuk	$40	$85
Tripoli	$60–65	$100
Constantinople and Smyrna	$90–100	$130

Sources: J. Richardson, *Narrative of a Mission to Central Africa*, etc. (2 volumes, London, 1853) Vol. II, pp. 202–4; D. C. Tambo, 'The Sokoto Caliphate Slave Trade in the Nineteenth Century'. *International Journal of African Historical Studies*, Vol. 9, 1976, pp. 187–217, Appendix.

Young girls were sold at the chief Hausa market at Kano for the equivalent of $32.[26] Boys were sold for one third as much. By the time slave-girls reached Murzuk, the per capita costs of travel, taxes and merchants' profits brought the price up to $85 ($40 for boys), while the relatively east journey to Tripoli gave them a market value there of around $100 ($60–65 dollars for boys). Their shipment on the Mediterranean 'middle passage' raised their final sale price at the great 'imperial' cities of Constantinople and Smyrna to $130, with up to $100 paid for boys. Thus between Kano and Constantinople or Smyrna, the gross profit on males was around $90 each on an initial outlay of only $8–12. Corresponding

24 J. Richardson, *Travels in the Great Desert of Sahara in the Years 1845 and 1846*, (2 Vols, London, 1848), Vol. II, pp. 115–9
25 J. Wright, 'The Wadai–Benghazi Slave Route', op. cit., p. 179
26 The Spanish Dollar, still in wide circulation in Africa and the Mediterranean, was exchanged at up to 5 for £1 Sterling, depending on location.

figures for girls were a $100 gross profit on a $30 initial outlay. While the greatest gross profit on both sexes was made on the longest and most difficult Saharan stage between the Sudanese entrepots and Murzuk, the trade in males became relatively more profitable the further they were moved from central Africa.

But net profits tell a rather different tale. The costs of taking slaves across the desert from Kano to Tripoli; taxes and unofficial but very necessary 'presents'; the expenses of maintaining slaves and presenting them decently at markets; then their shipping charge across the Mediterranean to Turkey – all these amounted to about $40 per head for both sexes in the 1840s.[27] Thus the more cooperative female trade slaves brought in higher net profits than the more troublesome trade in men and boys. On the trade between Hausaland and Constantinople, net profits were sixty per cent of gross profits for males, but nearly seventy per cent for women and girls.

All these prices and profits refer to the ordinary, young, unskilled and untrained trade slave. It is worth noting that by comparison, the English navvy -that hard-drinker, champion fighter and prodigiously hard-working tough who dug the canals of Britain and then built the railways of Britain and the Continent - was calculated to have been worth £245 at age twenty-one, in terms of capital invested it him since birth, and £350 at his fully-skilled prime, aged thirty. He was thus as valuable as two race horses or two first-class carriage horses – say twenty-five to thirty-five raw trade slaves at a mid-Saharan mart.[28] As North African horses were traditionally traded in and beyond the Sahara for around fifteen slaves each, these calculations seem to be remarkably accurate.[29]

---

27 Wright, 'Nothing Else but Slaves', op. cit., Table 7.6, 'Expenses of Moving Slaves Hausa–Constantinople'

28 These were the calculations of the contemporary reformer and barrister Edwin Chadwick in the mid-1840s. On the basis of what he called contract prices for maintenance and education at a weekly rate of 4s. 6d. from birth, the capital invested in each man would actually have been £245 14s. at age 21, and not at age 20 as quoted in T. Coleman, *The Railway Navvies: A History of the Men Who Made the Railways*, (Harmondsworth, 1970), p. 142.

29 According to Leo Africanus in the sixteenth century, fifteen or sometimes twenty slaves were given for one horse in Bornu. (J. Pory, *A Geographical Historie of Africa, Written in Arabicke and Italian by John Leo a More etc.*, London, 1600), p. 293.); Lyon, *A Narrative*, p. 154.

Vice consul Gagliuffi calculated that the 2,900 slaves traded through Murzuk in 1854 were worth a total of £34,820, or an average of £12 ($60) each, the average having been lowered by the large number of men and boys in that year's consignments. There was also a traffic in some more expensive slaves – eunuchs or girls of exceptional beauty or talents – who were sold privately in closed houses, and were thus probably excluded from vice consul Gagliuffi's calculations. Add to this the market in a little gold dust, some ivory and senna pods, and the trade of Murzuk for 1854 may have amounted in all to as much as £40,000. It is quite likely that this trade had not increased all that much in value since it acquired its "modern" form in the early Islamic centuries. But what may have appeared as a rich and notable traffic by the meaner economic standards of the middle ages made little impression on the expanding global commerce of the mid-nineteenth century. Even by the 1840s, before the opening of the up-river traffic, Liverpool's palm oil trade with the Niger delta alone was worth at least ten times the whole year's business of a leading mid-Saharan market such as Murzuk.[30]

---

30 C. W. Newbury, *British Politics towards West Africa: Select Documents, 1786–1874*, (London, 1965), pp. 111–2

A GIFT TO THOSE WHO CONTEMPLATE THE WONDERS OF CITIES AND THE MARVELS OF TRAVELLING

DR ABDELHADI TAZI

HE Moroccan Monarch Sultan Abou-Inan was known the world over for his pioneering initiatives as recorded in the various archives in Africa, Europe and the East.

At the local level he established academic and cultural institutions which are still alive and operational. At a more personal level he had a reputation for having original and meaningful interest in literature and arts.

In 756H, corresponding to 1355AD, he decided to have the Travels of Ibn Battuta recorded. It was a relevant and constructive decision which reflected his insight as well as his appreciation for creativeness and free thought. He therefore ignored the speculations of those who were trying to cast doubt on the credibility of the 'Rihla' (Travel) which was mentioned by Ibn Khaldoun in the Prolegomena. Indeed, it is thanks to this decision that Sultan Abu-Inan's name has remained for ever associated throughout the world with the travels of Ibn Battuta.

Reports of the 'Rihla' were recounted in some publications in the Maghreb and the Middle East. They also aroused the interest of more and more scholars in different parts of the world.

Eventually, the German Orientalist Burckhardt discovered the 'Muntaqa', a selection of excerpts from the 'Rihla' as reported by Al Bayluni el-Halabi in 1085H corresponding to 1674AD.

After publications of some chapters of 'Muntaqa' in the early nineteenth century, the full text of the 'Rihla' was issued in French along with the Arabic version in France by Deferemery and Sanghinetti on the basis of three manuscripts which were available in the Paris-based Royal

Library.

This initiative encouraged Sir Hamilton Gibb to undertake the English translation of the 'Rihla'. His work was taken up and completed by his colleague Beckingham. The book was translated subsequently into about twenty languages.

However it was not until 1871 that the 'Rihla' was published in the Arab world. It was based on the Paris edition. In fact all subsequent editions in Cairo and Beyrouth relied basically on this Paris edition despite its flaws. We noticed that some publishers had taken some liberty with the original text by introducing deletions, rearrangements and additions.

I then realised it was my duty to authenticate such a significant portion of our heritage, especially after the Academy of the Kingdom of Morocco decided to publish the 'Rihla'.

In my investigations I came to consult thirty manuscripts. I made the necessary additions and corrected the various mistakes. I was also able to ascertain hundreds of geographical names and identify hundreds of prominent personalities whose names the 'Traveller' had recorded over the years. The work was compiled in five books, the last of which was devoted to more than thirty references and indexes. In addition I studied some twenty maps and a large number of drawings in an attempt to bring the reader closer to the reality as observed by Ibn Battuta when he visited more than a third of the countries which are today members of the United Nations Organisation!

Eventually it became clear that the famous Venetian Traveller' Marco Polo had actually covered much less ground than his counterpart from Tangiers who was then referred to as 'the Traveller among Arabs and non-Arabs alike' and as 'the rover who crossed the provinces lengthwise and widthwise'. Nowadays he is depicted as the 'greatest Traveller of all times'.

Ibn Battuta, the greatest globetrotter in the history of mankind

The autobiography of this illustrious man has been embedded in his own prolific account about his travels since he had left Tangier in 725AH (1325AD) and until he was received by Sultan Abou-Inan, in Fez, in Shaabane 750H (November 1349AD), on the occasion of his return, in the aftermath of which he embarked on a new peregrination to Andalucia, then to the Sudan.

Yet, some thirteen years in the life of this great man remain unknown. No information is disclosed on his conditions, nor on his household, except some news about the injunction made by Sultan Abou Inan to Ibn Juzay, the clerk in 757H (1356AD) to write down the account of Ibn Battuta's travels. Ibn Battuta was appointed later on as judge in the Tamesna Province one of the most affluent regions in the Kingdom of Bani Marin, situated between Bouregreg and Oum Rabii rivers.

But his voice died away following the death of his patron Sultan Abou-Inan in 759H (1356AD).

Born in Tangier on Monday 17 Rajab 703H. (24 February 1304AD), he died while still in office as judge in 770H (1356AD).

Ibn Battuta had embarked on many travels, interspersed with multifarious ordeals, and daunting perils too. But he came unscathed from all these terrifying experiences. So goes the saying, 'Only age kills'.

But some people go so far as to belittle Ibn Battuta, decrying, him as a man of limited culture. Their view is downright erroneous, since Ibn Battuta was a genuinely cultured man in the deepest sense of culture.

As you skim through the account of his peregrinations, you can realise these facts right from the first passage, as he was bidding farewell to Morocco, when his companions chose him as their judge.

Whether in Arabian or Persian land, he availed himself of the opportunity to delve into knowledge, and to knit ties with a large number of Sheikhs and scholars, women and men alike, who awarded him unreservedly their recommendations, which entitled him to take up the office of judge in India and the Maldives. Worth noting in Ibn Battuta's peregrinations is the fact that, in spite of his long absence and the many posts he held, he had never forgotten his homeland, Morocco, which remained ever engraved in his mind. He mentioned Ceuta whilst in Sanoub on the banks of the Black Sea. The images of the great Moroccan rivers always filled his mind, making him compare in one instance the Salé River with Istanbul Bosphorus. He took great pride in his Moroccan identity and was keen on giving vent to such a feeling.

Another point worth noting is the sharp sense with which he was endowed. His talks about prices, and his close follow-up of the situation of weights and measures as well as the value of currencies makes you feel you are reading a specialised newspaper chronicling market conditions.

One conspicuous fact about Ibn Battuta's amazing celerity of acclimatisation, for he would quickly learn the language of the folks he visited, he started assimilating Persian before he had command of the Turkish language because Persian was widespread in the region that extended to China. He used to transcribe these two languages in the Arabic script thus bearing testimony to the fact that the Arabic script is capable of assimilating all phonemes. This is an important scientific fact.

He was also eager to render accurately the geographical names describing them minutely to shun any spelling or pronunciation errors. This is one of the characteristics that distinguished our eminent globe-trotters from most geographers who had recorded geographical names. It is therefore only natural that his travels should be considered as a vivid geographical glossary that no researcher in the history of Africa, Asia or even southern Europe can do without.

One of the reasons that aroused my interest in Ibn Battuta's travels was the overriding feeling that infused my heart upon joining the United Nations' conference on the standardisation of geographical names, which is subsidiary to the Economic and Social Council of the United Nations in New York.

The goal of that conference was to survey and standardise geographical sites throughout the world. This was an auspicious occasion for me to correct, from the lofty international podium, about one thousand geographical names mentioned in Ibn Battuta's travels about the three continents he had visited.

The social conditions of women and their status in the nations he had visited prompted him to formulate interesting ideas about the situation of women. He spoke about chastity and compassion of the Khurasan women as well as the lofty status of Turkey and Tartar women to the extent that the enforcement of crucial decisions hinged on the approval of 'eminent ladies' side by side with sultans. He also talked about women in the desert and the Sudan, when the women used to enjoy her right to an equitable treatment.

We must mention here that whenever Marco Polo the Venetian was mentioned, the scholars concerned with travels and travellers always talked about Ibn Battuta, the man from Tangiers. Marco Polo had visited the Far East some sixty years before, and his memoirs, which were recorded afterwards, were the object of extensive comments. Yet, it is worth noting that the scope of Ibn Battuta's travels was larger than Marco Polo's, in addition to the contrasting inherent scientific value of both.

While Ibn Battuta had embarked on his travels alone, and the writer of his travel account (Ibn Juzay) was highly trustworthy in the rendition of his travels, it must be noted that Rustichello., the writer of Marco Polo's travels, used to supplement the travel accounts with figments of his imagination. We have today the English translation, published in 1818 by William Marsden, from the original Italian text published by Ramusio in 1559.

After Marsden, other editions appeared, with many additions. They totalled over one hundred editions, all dissimilar, while Ibn Battuta's travels have remained as they first appeared in the Fez edition of 757H (1356AD).

While voicing his pride on his unparalleled, far-reaching travels, Ibn Battuta pointed out that he had surpassed the Egyptian traveller Sheikh Abdullah who had neither gone to China, nor to Sardanib Island, Morocco, Andalusia or the Sudan. I personally believe that had Ibn Battuta met with Marco Polo, he would have made the same comment. For we know that the lands visited by that traveller from Tangiers surpass by far those crossed by Marco Polo.

But our traveller from Tangiers excels the Venetian traveller in another essential matter. He managed to mingle with the local population through marriage as well as through the top-ranking offices he held and the close contacts he made with different circles. Such dynamism fulfilled his curiosity and met his ever -renewed aspirations. To know the calibre of both men and gauge the cognitive input in their works, suffice it to survey the number of geographical names mentioned in their works, and sort out the proper names cited in their memoirs. We will then certainly find ourselves paying tribute to the tremendous memory of the Moroccan traveller who managed to memorise such a considerable number of geographical and proper names, in spite of the plunder of his memoirs in the Indian Ocean. Such a power of assimilation and recollection is, indeed, beyond human capacity. Similarly, when it comes to the exotic, novel elements in both travel, it can be safely upheld, without hesitation, that Ibn Battuta had excelled Marco Polo, his counterpart.

This period in history teemed with travels made by renowned globetrotters. From the Western world, apart from Marco Polo, there was also Odoric who visited Asia immediately after Polo. As from the Arab world, there were Ahmed Ben Fadlan, Ibn Jubayr al-Ahdalusi, al-Abdari al-Hihi and Abu Hamed al-Gharnati. Yet, with its far-reaching surface, its long duration and its extensive input, Ibn Battuta travel surpasses all those.

One day, as I was speaking about Ibn Battuta, I said to my fellow member in the Academy of the Kingdom of Morocco, Mr Neil Armstrong, (the man who had gone to the moon): 'Ibn Battuta is one of your fellow explorers.' His reply was quite simple: 'There is a huge difference between us. Whereas I was pushed into a machine, then I found myself on the moon, and was told to go back afterwards, I realized that Ibn Battuta, during his thirty-year peregrinations, had been walking all the way through, or at times riding a horse, a camel, an elephant, a cart, a sedan or a ship in order to achieve his exploration goals.' Clear then that Ibn Battuta's travels are the first of their kind in the history of the entire mankind, as upheld by a large number of researchers.

HOW AND WHY THE TUAREG POISONED THE FRENCH.

Some reflections on efelehleh and the motives of the Tuareg in massacring the Flatters expedition of 1881

JEREMY KEENAN

HERE are many written accounts of the doomed Flatters mission. They vary slightly on points of detail – precise distances, directions, names of places, numbers of personnel and camels and so forth – which is not surprising since the story of what happened to the expedition was recounted to the French authorities almost three months after disaster overtook it and by a small group of survivors whose memories were quite possibly tarnished by experiences which had sent most of their colleagues to delirium, death or both. I will recount the story again here, for it loses nothing of its horror in the retelling, and without being able to add anything more to it other than to throw some interesting light (for those who do not already know it) on the nature of the poisonous herb – efelehleh – that was used by the Tuareg against their unfortunate victims. And, of course, there are still a few lingering questions about the motives that lay behind the Tuareg's actions and on which I shall try and throw some light.

In every respect – conception, planning, execution and outcome, the Flatters expedition of 1880–1 that set out to reconnoitre a route for a railway across the Sahara was a total disaster. Indeed, it is a matter of eternal debate whether Flatters himself or his sponsors in Paris were the most incompetent.

The mood in France at the time was not conducive to clear thinking and sensible planning. The pretensions of the premier power in Europe had been shattered in the few short weeks of the Franco-Prussian War of 1870–71. Still smarting from the stinging defeat at the hands of Bismarck, the political atmosphere in Paris was one in which grandiose schemes and almost senseless reasoning had more than their fair share of expression. France wanted to strengthen and consolidate her hold over colonial territories. In particular she wanted a closer link with her Sudanese and West African territories and saw the answer in a trans-Saharan railway, a scheme proposed by Adolphe Duponchel, a civil engineer from Montpellier. In 1878 Duponchel had published a book, *The Transsaharian Railway*, which set off a wave of railway fever through the country. He argued that a railway would save endless time in the transportation of goods. The fact that the Americans had succeeded in building a railway across their continent eleven years previously merely gave further impetus to the scheme.

The three possible routes for the railway were: (1) the route more or less followed by René Caillé in 1828 across the flat expanse of Tanezrouft to the west of Ahaggar; (2) from Laghouat to Ouargla, across some dangerous sand-tracts, and then through the unknown and precipitous Hoggar (Ahaggar) mountains, (3) the ancient caravan route across the Fezzan from Tripoli to Lake Chad.

The arguments in favour of the Hoggar route, which was eventually chosen by Charles de Freycinet, the Minister of Public Works and later Prime Minister of France, were based largely on the fact that the extension of French territory as far as Ouargla would enable supplies and assistance to be rendered more quickly and easily, and the reports of the young French geographer, Henri Duveyrier, who in 1857 and at the young age of 18 had been the first European to travel amongst the northern Tuareg (although without actually entering Ahaggar). Young, intelligent, but a touch naïve, Duveyrier had reported on the friendliness of the Tuareg towards the French. In addition, M. de Freycinet also considered that the Tuareg would welcome these new facilities for trade, and totally ignored both the counsels of a commission that opposed any railway scheme on practical grounds, and the advice of the officers of the Bureaux des Affaires Indigènes, who pointed out that Tuareg preferred to raid rather than trade for their needs No consideration at all was given to such practicalities as to how the locomotive would be supplied with water, coal or wood in the midst of this barren desert.

The choice of Lt-Colonel Paul Flatters to lead the expedition was as defective and inappropriate as the rest of the thinking of the Transsaharian Committee, the body in Paris which was established to promote and oversee the project. In his book, *The Conquest of the Sahara*, Douglas Porch described the disparate assortment of people who comprised the Committee as: soldiers with some experience of the Sahara; geographers supposedly expert on the desert (but who had never actually been there) many of them from left-wing university circles and hostile to the *Africains* – soldiers whose primary service was in Algeria, engineers long on technical knowledge but extremely naïve about desert conditions; a sprinkling of chamber-of-commerce types with Algerian interests; and politicians with their own axes to grind and constituencies to defend.'

At first glance, Flatters might have seemed the ideal candidate to lead the expedition. He was an army officer with some twenty years experience of Algeria and the Arab Bureau – created to administer the North African population, and he spoke Arabic. The Transsaharian Committee was also no doubt impressed by his apparent knowledge of North Africa and its peoples. In 1863, he wrote a book: *Histoire ancienne du Nord de l'Afrique avant le conquete des Arabes.* The book was directed at an Arab audience. Two years later he dressed it up for a European market under the title *Histoire de la géographie et géologie de la province de Constantine.* Finally, in 1879, he published *Etude sur l'Afrique septentrionale des origins à l'invasion arabe* in the academically prestigious *Revue historique.* He had also written three reports for the government on the caravan trade between the Mediterranean and the Sudan. Although his writings did not bear the hallmark of either great scholarship or intellect, they undoubtedly impressed the Committee, to whom he must have appeared as the obvious expert on the desert and its problems.

What the Committee did not know, and probably could not have known, when they fished him out of his far off desert outpost in Laghouat and asked him to give his views on the feasibility of laying a rail track from Algiers to the Sudan, was that his long isolation in the Arab Bureau, dealing almost entirely with local administrative affairs, had undermined his ability to command. He was a man of apparent over-weight, ill-health – he had long suffered acute sciatica – and suffering, so one might suggest – at the age of forty-eight – a certain middle age disillusionment with life. Perhaps he saw the Committee and its extra-vagant ideas as his one opportunity to revive his career and write his name into the history books.

The expedition that left Ouargla on 5 March 1880 – later to become known as 'The First Expedition' – was a pretty motley crew. It comprised some 111 persons: twenty-five Frenchmen, eight of whom were from a penal battalion, two *spahis* from the Arab Bureau, two Arab cooks, twelve guides and seventy Chaamba cameleers. I will not go into the details of this First Expedition here, other than to say that it soon disintegrated into abject disorder and disarray. Within two weeks, Flatters and the French had lost command and control of the expedition. The Chaamba had effectively revolted, saying that they were not prepared to head towards Ahaggar, the land of their lifelong and much-feared enemies – the Tuareg. Flatters's brief was to head into Ahaggar. But, rather than return to Ouargla, he gave in to the Chaamba and headed towards Ghat – territory quite unsuitable for the proposed railway as it was claimed by Turkey. He soon found his path blocked by Tuareg and on 21 April finally ordered a retreat.

One of the more intriguing aspects of Flatters's second expedition was how he ever managed to persuade the Transsaharian Committee to back it. In today's world, Flatters would probably be regarded as something between a misguided fool and a con man. Somehow he managed to hide the whole débâcle of the first expedition from the Committee. What he told the Committee was nothing more than a pack of lies. He managed to persuade them that he had been made most welcome by the Kel Ahaggar Tuareg (Kel = people of); that he had not met the slightest opposition and that the expedition had been seen as 'the crowning act of friendliness and of good neighbourliness between Algerian Chaamba and Tuareg'.[1] The reason for his turning back, he told the Committee, was because to proceed without first obtaining permission from both Turk and Tuareg might have raised a diplomatic issue. And the reason why he had not been able to wait any longer to get this permission was because he did not have sufficient provisions to care for the Tuareg who had come to join him!

It was clear to anyone who had had even a glimpse of what happened on that first expedition that Flatters was unfit for command. He was also an ill man when he set out from Laghouat on the second expedition in November of that same year. According to one report,[2] his sciatica had flared up again, requiring up to four shots of morphine each day as well as 'cauterisations with a hot iron. ' He could not walk for more than thirty minutes and was comfortable only in a reclining position.

1   R. Pottier, *Flatters*, Paris 1948.
2   ibid. (quoted by Douglas Porch, *The Conquest of the Sahara*, 1984).

Flatters's second expedition comprised either ninety-three or ninety-seven personnel, the difference being attributable to how various reports on the expedition counted the Chaamba guides and cameleers. Some reports say that there were thirty-one Chaamba guides and cameleers, others that there were thirty-one cameleers and seven guides. The precise number is of no consequence and with the general coming and going of the cameleers and guides, the precise number was probably never known. In addition to the Chaamba, there were forty-seven Arab Tirailleurs and eleven Frenchmen. The Frenchmen were Flatters himself, Captain Pierre Masson, Lieutenant Joseph Dianeaux (de Dianous), Sergeants Dennery and Joseph Pobéquin, Private Brame and five engineers: Emile Béringer, Jules Roche, Dr (Major) Robert Guiard and two civilians, Santin and Marjolet.

One other person to accompany the expedition was a holy *mokhadem*, whose attachment to the expedition gives rise to an amusing anecdote. The expedition set off from Laghouat, which is close to the headquarters of the Tidjani sect. A few years before, in the 1870s, the head of the sect, Si Ahmed, who was fabulously wealthy, had married a young French girl – Aurélie Picard – and she had set up her home in Laghouat. While Flatters seems to have been fairly gung-ho about the expedition, his confidence was not shared by the remaining Frenchmen. As for the Chaamba, they knew only too well the dangers they faced at the hands of the Tuareg, and were openly fearful.

Aurélie decided to boost French courage by holding a grand dinner on the eve of the expedition's departure. Serving them the finest champagne, she tried to rally their spirits and their courage, telling them it was imperative that they penetrate the legendary land of the Tuareg, otherwise it would remain forever barred to France. To overcome the fears of the Chaamba and the other Arab auxiliaries, Aurélie arranged for a *mokhadem* of the Tidjani order to be attached to the expedition. The *mokhadem*, she said, would ensure the safety of the Moslem members of the expedition, and also that of the infidels, for the influence of the Tidjanis extended over the whole Sahara, as far as the river Niger, and not even the Tuareg, said Aurélie, would dare molest a Tidjani holy man.

Recently, when I was travelling in Ahaggar with a Tuareg friend, we began discussing the story of Flatters's expedition. When I recounted Aurélie's contribution, my Tuareg friend remarked: 'That sounds like the right recipe for courage: alcohol for one and religion for the other!'

Flatters had already written to the supreme chief (*Amenukal*) of the Tuareg, Aitarel, not so much asking for his permission to travel through Ahaggar as more or less announcing his attention to pass through the country regardless of the Tuareg. There is something of a mystery surrounding Flatters's declared intentions. He had announced that he was going to lead his expedition to In Salah in the Touat, an area which was firmly under the control of the Kel Ahaggar. In fact, as he told his wife, he had no intention of going near In Salah. His announcement, he explained to her, was a deception, designed, so he thought, to make the Touat prepare to resist him, so that the expedition could more easily go about its business elsewhere. Such an announcement, whatever its questionable motives, was not the most brilliant act of diplomacy for its effect was almost certainly to make the Tuareg even more determined to resist him, irrespective of what route he planned to follow.

Aitarel's reply, stating that the column would not be allowed through Ahaggar, was brushed aside contemptuously and the arrogant colonel resolutely headed the column south. The Chaamba were especially nervous and Flatters threatened to shoot any who opposed him. On 10 January the Chaamba became even more alarmed when at the wells of El Dadjadj they ran into a small northbound caravan which confirmed Aitarel's hostility to the mission.

Flatters refused to head the warnings of his guides and even his own officers who begged him to show caution. A few days later, on 18 January 1881, they reached the Amguid gorge, one of two passages into Ahaggar from the north. The expedition stayed at Amguid, where there was good water, for five days. Flatters found it a sinister place and his comments, made in a letter to his wife, give a small clue to his concerns and state of mind: 'We are at this moment at the foot of a mountain of enormous rocks, cut by a gorge at the bottom of which runs a stream. The first running water we have met in the Sahara! There are fish in the water, but it seems a bad sign: There were also fish in the lake[3] where we ended our last voyage. Will the fish inadvertently bring us bad luck?'[4]

3   This is a reference to Lake Menghough, north of Ghat.
4   Pottier, op cit. (quoted by Douglas Porch, *The Conquest of the Sahara*, 1984).

The expedition left Amguid on 23 January. They were now entering the preserve of the Kel Ahaggar Tuareg, land that was unknown to his Chaamba guides.

A few days later, on 25 January, they were met by a mounted Tuareg bearing a letter from Aitarel stating that the rider had been sent on his authority to escort the column into Ahaggar. Flatters, naively unsuspicious of any treachery, became even more confident as seemingly friendly veiled warriors assured him of Aitarel's friendliness. Only the Chaamba, worried by the multitude of tracks that crossed and recrossed their path, and familiar with the ways of their traditional enemies, remained suspicious of this uncustomary friendliness, and, convinced that they were being led into a trap, begged Flatters to allow them to return home. Flatters refused, but, as they moved deeper into Ahaggar, condescended to post double sentries at night.

Flatters's precise route immediately south of Amguid is not clear to me. My own inclination is that the expedition would have been heading due south up the Oued Irharhar towards the Garet el Djenoun at the northern end of the Tefedest. His planned route certainly seems to have been towards the southwest, and his description of the mountains and rocks they passed sound very much like the Tefedest, although they could conceivably have been parts of the Tourha mountains through which he would certainly have passed at some point in order to reach the Plain of Amadror. Flatters himself was not completely taken in: he was suspicious of the guides who kept telling him they were lost and he could see from his compass that they were being taken in a south easterly direction when he had wanted to go towards the southwest.

His route took him across the desolate Plain of Amadror and, by my reckoning, into the more mountainous area south of Amadror, probably between Djebel Telertheba and Mount Serkout. As the days progressed, the column became more aware of the presence of Tuareg and likely treachery. On 16 February the expedition set off at dawn, only for the accompanying Tuareg guides to inform Flatters that they had missed the wells. After changing course and crossing a stony plain interspersed with patches of sand, they arrived, a little before midday, at a spot where recent rain had left a few pools of water. Here they made camp.

What follows next varies slightly in detail according to different sources. But the general line of events is fairly clear. As there was insufficient water for all the animals, the Tuareg guides suggested that the colonel, with some of the officers and the cameleers should leave the camp and take the animals to a place called Tadjemout, about two hours away, where there was ample water for the animals and their water-skins. Flatters agreed and set off with the Tuareg guides, accompanied by Captain Masson and the engineers Béringer, Roche and Guiard. A small group of Chaamba and Tirailleurs brought the bulk of the camels, while Sergeant Dennery, with about twenty Tirailleurs formed a covering rearguard.

Flatters had foolishly allowed the column to be divided. Some forty or so men had gone with the colonel, about forty-five, including Dianeaux, Pobéguin, Santin, Marjolet and Brame, remained in the camp. Even when one of the Tuareg guides told Flatters that he had been betrayed, he still refused to heed the warning.

At the wells the animals were led away to drink and the small party rested in the shade of the tamarisk trees. But the peaceful scene did not last for long. Tuareg, waiting in ambush, charged down on the small party and slaughtered the entire group, hacking most of them to death with their swords, although not before several had fallen under the Frenchmen's desperate fire. The rearguard of Tirailleurs reached the crest of the hill overlooking the wells in time only to witness the final scenes of the massacre. The camels had already been driven off into the mountains and about one hundred Tuareg, now armed with the rifles taken from the dead cameleers, had been left to guard the wells. In spite of such odds Sergeant Dennery and his band of Tirailleurs held their ground, killing several Tuareg, until, with his ammunition running low and casualties mounting, he called off the attack. But with the sound of gunfire attracting ever-increasing numbers of Tuareg the retreat to the main camp was a hazardous business, and Dennery himself died in the attempt. Under constant harassment, ten of the original party fought their way back to join their companions.

For the forty desperate survivors, now under the command of Lieutenant Dianeaux, there was no alternative but to face an impossible trek back to the nearest French post – Ouargla – eight hundred miles to the north. With no transport each man would have to carry his own rifle, ammunition, water and food supplies, with little hope of replenishment and under constant harassment from the Tuareg shadowing their flanks.

When the supply of rice was finished the men began to chew leather; two Saluki dogs accompanying the expedition were killed for meat, and a wild ass was shot and eaten raw.

In their desperate plight many of the Tirailleurs wanted to commit suicide, but the French maintained a degree of optimism which was raised when four stray camels were found and taken to relieve the men of their loads. The column was under constant surveillance from the Tuareg, who even came to sell a few mangy camels for exorbitant sums of money. In ten days they had progressed a mere one hundred and ten miles.

The little group of survivors pressed on northwards, but they were still to the south of Amguid, and they new that such a strategic site, with its abundant water supply, would not be left unguarded. On 9 March, three weeks after the massacre, they reached the wells of Ain el Kerma, beneath the western scarp of Ahellakane and only a few hours from Amguid. The wells were occupied by about a hundred Tuareg. Dianeaux ordered them to leave, which they did, only to occupy a ridge a short distance away. Pobéguin was for launching an attack, but the lieutenant refused. After a while, one of the Tuareg came forward and threw down two bags of crushed dates with the promise of sheep on the next day if their price was met.

The starving men had scarcely devoured more than a few mouthfuls when they collapsed on the ground, foaming at the mouth and raving like maniacs. The crushed dates had been mixed with *efelehleh*, a most dangerous plant. When taken in small doses its sends a person delirious; slightly larger doses are lethal. Fortunately, the Chaamba were suspicious of such generosity and did not touch the dates; they were consequently able to subdue their raving colleagues, some of whom had rushed off into the desert never to return, while others, including Lieutenant Dianeaux, in their delirium, were tearing off their clothes and shooting each other.

Why the Tuareg did not attack their victims when they were in this helpless state is a mystery. We can only surmise whether it was an act of pure sadism, a desire to continue the game of cat and mouse and watch the drawn-out agony; whether it was to prevent any further loss of their own lives in open attack when the remainder of the booty would assuredly be theirs for the taking in a matter of time, or whether it was a carefully designed act of cruelty, which, when reported to the French authorities, possibly by a few 'permitted'; survivors, would act as a deterrent against further violation of their territorial sovereignty.

The next ploy was to sell the column the promised sheep, but on the condition that responsible men were sent to negotiate the deal. Dianeaux, feeling that the Tuareg would have some respect for the holy *mokhadem*, delegated him and three other men who had not been affected by the poisoned dates to act as emissaries.

The Tuareg were grouped on the edge of a cliff overlooking the approach to the Amguid gorge. As the *mokhadem* and three Chaamba soldiers approached they were seized and bound, and lined up against the cliff in sight of their companions. The three Chaarnba were decapitated in turn. Then, after a short pause, the *mokhadem* was split in half from skull to hips with a heavy broadsword.[5] Once again, Pobéguin wanted to attack, but was restrained by Dianeaux, who, although still semi-comatosed, realised that he could do nothing as the Tuareg were keeping well out of rifle range. Instead, he ordered the remainder of his men to continue the advance to the precious water of Amguid. As they had suspected, it was heavily guarded and Dianeaux, much to his credit, led a well-organised attack that inflicted heavy casualties on the Tuareg and drove them out of the gorge. In battling to the water, however, Dianeaux gave his life, along with Private Brame and the civil engineer, Marjolin. His colleague Santin had already died from the *efelehleh*.

Command of the little group of stragglers – thirty-four Tirailleurs and Chaamba – now fell to Sergeant Pobéguin, a cavalryman and the last surviving Frenchman, who was so ill from the effects of the *efelehleh* that he had to be carried on an already overladen camel. Although most of the men were still suffering the effects of the poisoned dates, they somehow staggered relentlessly northwards.

On 11 March four Tirailleurs deserted. Miraculously they made it back to Ouargla. At least two others were to follow their example, but without their good fortune.

On 18 March, almost five weeks after the death of Flatters, they reached one of the camps they had set up in January, where they found the parched remains of a dead camel. The bones and dried skin were all that they now had left to eat, and although they had miraculously

5   Some reports say that five Chaamba were killed.

struggled this far they knew they could not reach safety unless they found more food.

What happened during the next two weeks reads in the official report like a horror story. Pobéguin was a dying invalid; discipline no longer existed, and each man was on his own. On 22 March they reach the wells of Hassi el-Hakjadj where one of the Tirailleurs volunteered to go in search of the camp of one of original guides. He was followed by three other Tirailleurs who left camp on the pretext of hunting gazelles. Those that remained behind heard shots and when one of the hunters returned carrying meat it was soon recognised as the flesh of the volunteer who had been killed and devoured by the starving men.

After three days at the wells, Pobéguin summoned his energy and authority and ordered the remaining men to continue their march. Nine were unable to move and were left at the well. Only sixteen men accompanied Pobéguin northwards. They had not gone far when they heard shots from the direction of the well, the cook, Private Belkacem ben-Zebla was sent to investigate. What happened at the well will never be know. Belkacem returned carrying a quantity of human flesh which was apparently eaten raw. Even Pobéguin joined his men in the meal while some of the group returned to the wells to eat what had been left there.

Cannibalism was now the accepted means of survival; Belkacem, in addition to the task of preparing the meat, took upon himself the role of official executioner. His companions were now specimens of professional interest, and on the following day he summarily executed and roasted two more men. In fear, all eyes stayed pinned on Belkacem, none daring to sleep even for a moment.

Pobéguin was still alive, but only just, and discussion now centred on whether to save him from further suffering and so render assistance to his companions. The thought of butchering a Frenchman elicited considerable discussion, particularly from El Madani, the last surviving Tirailleur NCO, who retained his respect for a Frenchman of superior rank, but Belkacem settled the issue by shooting Pobéguin without further ado.

On the next day they at last came across a nomadic camp where they rested for two days before hiring camels to take them to Ouargla, and on 4 April 4, about two months after leaving the scene of the Flatters's massacre, El Madani led eleven half-dead Chaamba into the town.

The story of the Flatters still haunts the Sahara. It is difficult to stand in the gorge at Amguid without imagining the site of the *mokhadem* being cut in two, or to cross Amadror without thinking of the treachery that lead Flatters to his death. But the one thing that had long intrigued me was *efelehleh*. What did it look like? What was the poison and where in Ahaggar was it found?

On several occasions Tuareg had told me of a few places where it grew. But it was only last year, 2000, that I finally found myself travelling with a group of Tuareg in an area where *efelehleh* was known to flourish. The spot, ironically, was almost certainly crossed by Flatters and might well have been the place from which the *efelehleh* that was used to poison the survivors of the massacre had been collected. The spot was a wide, shallow oued on the western side of Amadror. None of my companions knew the name of the Oued, which was between the old salt workings of Tisemt at the southern end of the Oued Amadror and Djebel Amzer Oumfat in the Tourha. We had arrived there in the late afternoon after travelling over a black-and-white patchwork of salt deposits and lava. The lava looked as though a few million medium-sized lumps of coal, fallen from a flotilla of lorries, had been raked out to make a level surface. Had the patches been perfect squares, we might have been travelling over a giant chess board. The oued gave the whole landscape an even more surreal look, cutting a great swathe of deep bottle green across the chess board.

Since first reading about the Flatters expedition I had become almost obsessed by *efelehleh*. I was now staring at literally thousands of specimens of this most obnoxious looking plant, none of which was more than about sixty centimetres high, with the larger specimens being about a hundred and fifty centimetres across. Quite apart from their virulent colour and foetid smell, the very shape of the plants was off-putting, its fleshy, upward-pointing leaves giving it a spiky, grasping appearance. Amid the green foliage lurked scant numbers of tiny purple flowers. I examined it closely, walking from one specimen to the other, and as I did so became aware of a curious rustling noise, which I assumed was being made by a sort of cricket. Then I noticed that almost every plant was shrouded in spiders' webs. The sound must have come from the spiders, scuttling about in the dry sandy depths of the plants. It was quite a shock, for suddenly I remembered an obscure report I had once come across, on the use of this plant in India, which noted that people who had been poisoned by it (and, presumably, survived) had reported hallucinations of being chased by knee-high spiders!

Efelehleh's botanical name is *Hyoscyamus muticus* subspecies *falezlez*, a member of the potato family, the *Solonaceae*, which also includes the deadly nightshade. Its closest relative is henbane, *H. niger*, known to the French as *la jusquiame*. In his French-Tamahak dictionary, Foucauld referred to it as *la jusquiame de l'Ahaggar*. The reason for its name *niger is* because of the colour of its seeds, but wholly appropriate to its long association with witchcraft and death; another common name is 'corpse flower'. In fact, the extremities and swellings of people poisoned by it often turn quite black.

Members of the Solonaceae family probably contain a greater and more dangerous cocktail of alkaloids than any other plants on earth – atropine, scopolamlne, datura and L-hyosoyamine, amongst others. The symptoms of poisoning by *efelehleh* – the Solonaceae – are almost endless, and grotesque: fits of frenzy, convulsions and delirium; blocking of the functioning of the sweat glands making heat regulation of the body impossible, leading to coma and respiratory paralysis; hyperthermia burning skin and fiery rashes – (giving the urge to undress) followed by desquamation; complete cessation of mental faculties, vertigo, dizziness; burning eyes; sensation of scalding to lips and tongue; swollen and burning throat; and so on. The list is almost endless. Every part of the body is affected, mostly in the most painful and grotesque ways, with the usual outcome being death.

The descriptions we have of the victims of Flatters's expedition fit perfectly with those found in the specialist works on plants poisons and their medicinal properties. The survivors who made it back to Ouargla had not exaggerated.

When we had arrived at the oued we found a herd of about fifty gazelles grazing on the *efelehleh*. Gazelles and many other animals graze on it quite safely, but humans eating their stomachs and intestines can be taken seriously ill. Tuareg have been known to die in this way. We took one for the pot and I watched attentively as the gazelle was prepared, noting the careful disposal of its stomach and innards.

In telling the story of the Flatters mission, one is always left with the question of ' Why'. What were the motives of the Kel Ahaggar in this ugly episode? One can understand that they did not want foreign intruders in their land. But why not just kill them directly? Why the long, tortuous game of cat and mice? And why allow a few survivors when they too could quite easily have been killed?

I can do little more than speculate on what may have been in the minds of men who are long since dead and who kept no written records of their thoughts or deeds. But, in spite of our meagre knowledge of the Tuareg at this time, we know enough of what was going on in Ahaggar to make a few suggestions about why they acted in this way.

The first thing we can say is that the attack on the Flatters expedition was not organised by the whole federation (*tegehe*) of the Kel Ahaggar. On the contrary, the massacre seems to have been the exclusive business of the two noble drum-groups, the Kel Rela and the Tegehe-Mellet. The third such group, the Taitok, was preoccupied elsewhere with counter-raids of their own. Also, and as I will suggest in a moment, it may well have been that the Flatters' massacre was embedded in the prevailing struggle for the position of *Amenkual*, which at that time had become a singularly Kel Rela affair. This probably explains Flatters's route. We know from his own records that after passing Amguid, Flatters wanted to head southwest. But his treacherous guides were taking him towards the southeast, away from the territory of the Taitok on the western side of Ahaggar and more into the territory that fell between the Kel Rela and Tegehe Mellet to the east of Ahaggar.

The second pertinent piece of information that we have is that the actual participants in the massacre seem to have represented an emergent faction within the Kel Rela. By 1900, twenty years after the massacre, Ahaggar was clearly split by 'pro' and 'anti' French fractions. There is evidence to suggest that these movements were jockeying for position and influence at the time of the Flatters expedition. Indeed, the timing of Flatters's push into Ahaggar is critical to our understanding of the events that overtook him. The key date is 1877, three years before his arrival. In that year the Amenukal El Hadj Akhmed died. To call him a great statesman is a bit far-fetched, but he was certainly a man of great intelligence, diplomacy and farsightedness. At his death, many of his qualities and much of his wisdom lived on in the person of Khyar ag Heguir, El Hadj Akhmed's stepson. Khyar grew up under the guiding eye of the great Amenukal and was closely associated with all matters of government. Khyar was very much his stepfather's protégé, but although he was of the right descent line (through his matriline) he was not directly in line to succeed to the position of Amenukal, which passed to El Hadj Akhmed's mother's sister's son, Aitarel.[6]

From the work of Maurice Benhazera,[7] we know that it was Khyar's ambition to become Amenukal, and we know that he felt frustrated in this respect and was constantly opposed by Aitarel. Frustration and jealousy no doubt contributed to Khyar's feelings towards Aitarel, but the opposition between them seems to have been more deep-rooted, stemming from a fundamental difference in policy. Khyar condemned the Flatters massacre and even went so far as to communicate his opinion to the French. It is doubtful whether this stance was made out of sheer antagonism towards Aitarel, for there are indications that Khyar may have been prepared to enter into negotiations with the French some two years earlier (at the end of war between the Kel Ajjer and Kel Ahaggar, 1875–8).[8] If he had been in command of Ahaggar. The extent to which Khyar advocated a more conciliatory and diplomatic policy towards the French is not known, but any gesture of conciliation by Aitarel might have been regarded as giving weight to Khyar's policy and thus strengthening his position in Ahaggar – something which the French would most certainly have welcomed. I am, of course, indulging in considerable speculation, but I suggest that Aitarel's decision not only to attack Flatters but to execute the attack in such a gruesome manner may well have been influenced by Khyar's opposition. An overwhelming victory over such a large and well-armed force of 'invading Christians', particularly if the number of casualties was relatively low, would have enhanced his position, not only through the prestige to be gained as a great strategist and 'defender' of Ahaggar, but also by reducing the attraction and credibility of Khyar's conciliatory policy.

If I am correct in this surmise then Aitarel must be credited with considerable astuteness, for the action checked any further encroachment on Ahaggar for nearly twenty years. Furthermore, although a certain

6   For details of the complex succession rules and the circumstances of the succession at this time, see Keenan, J., The Tuareg: People of Ahaggar, 1997 (republished, Sickle Moon Books, 2001)

7   Benhazera, M., Six Mois chez les Touareg du Ahaggar, Alger, 1908

8   see Keenan, J., op cit. pp. 63–72.

'pro-French' faction still centred around Khyar it held little weight, and Aitarel managed to maintain some semblance of authority over Ahaggar until his death in 1900.[9]

Finally, there is the question of how far Aitarel felt he was invoking a 'holy' war, as has sometimes been claimed. His letter to the Kaimakam of Ghadames,[10] quoted by Schirmer[11] is particularly interesting in this respect:

> Au nom de Dieu Clément et miséricordieux, écrivait-if, vous nous aviez recommendé de surveiller les routes et de les preserver contre les gens hostiles, c'est ce que nous avons fait. Aujourd'hui ne voilà-t-il pas que les Chrétiens veulent suivre nos routes! Ils sont venus dans l'Ahaggar, mais les gens de cette contrée les ont combattus pour la guerre sainte de la manière la plus énergique, les ont massacrés et c'est fini. Maintenant, il faut absolument, ô cher ami, que la nouvelle de nos hauts-faits parvienne à Constantinople. On dit que les Chrétiens sont énergiques et batailleurs, donc, ô cher ami, faites parvenir mes paroles à Constantinople et dites en haut lieu que je demande à ce que les musulmans viennent à notre aide pour soutenir la guerre sainte.

While the Tuareg were certainly intolerant of Christians, or any foreigner or outsider for that matter, they themselves have never been especially devout Moslems, and although there is no reason to doubt the authenticity of the letter, its pious tone is not becoming of a Tuareg and is suggestive of ulterior motivations. My own opinion, which is speculative, is that Islam merely provided Aitarel with a degree of legitimacy and a means of diverting attention from internal intrigues within Ahaggar. In addition, the letter may well have been designed to gain recognition from important Moslem leaders outside Ahaggar in order to enhance his

---

9　Khyar's position was epitomised later in the personage of Moussa ag Amastene, Amenukal from 1905–20, without whose lone support for the French against the Senussi revolt during the First World War the French position in the Sahara would probably have become untenable.

10　This was the Amrar Safi, who was appointed Kaimakam (a Turkish title) by the Turks on their arrival in Ghat.

11　Schirmer, H., *Le Sahara*, Paris, 1893, p. 393.

prestige and status in Ahaggar, as well as to secure foreign support in the case of French reprisals.

If I have speculated on the motives for the Tuareg action, at least its consequences are more clear. As far as the French were concerned, the shocking outcome of the Flatters expedition put a stop to any further penetration into the Central Sahara, at least until the end of the 1890s. In spite of the fact that four hundred armed Chaamba from Ouargla were placed immediately at the disposition of the French command, and that Khyar's feelings were well known, no reprisal action was carried out against the Tuareg. Such action could have proved acutely embarrassing and difficult for France at the international level and, as the military commander of the Cercle de Laghouat explained, revenge against the Tuareg, in the form of a military operation, would be a hazardous and uncertain business.

AMBASSADORS AND ENVOYS OF THE KINGDOM OF MOROCCO TO THE UNITED KINGDOM

An annotated chronological list from 1588 to 2000

MOHAMMED BELMAHI

Ambassador of his Majesty the King of Morocco to the Court of St James

THE first British diplomatic contact with the kingdom of Morocco dates from 1213 with the following envoys of King John: knight Thomas Hardington, and knight Ralph Fitz-Nicholas, accompanied by Robert of London, a clerk.

They were received in an audience by the monarch of Morocco, Mohammed en-Nassir of the Almohad dynasty, in the city of Marrakesh.[1]

This recorded contact is recognised as one of the earliest known events in the history of diplomatic relations of the United Kingdom with other nations.

As an illustration of this statement, Moroccan-British diplomatic relations were established over one hundred years prior to the first recorded exchange of ambassadors between the United Kingdom and France, dated in 1315.

In 1551, the first Moroccan diplomats (and also the first ever Muslim ones) arrived to London as representatives of their monarch, the Sa'adian Sultan Mohammed al-Shaykh (1540-57). They were 'two moors, being noble men, whereof one was of the kings blood '.[2] No names of these two diplomats seem to have survived to reach us.

However, a sustained exchange of known ambassadors and envoys between the Kingdom of Morocco and the United Kingdom started only with the respective reigns of Sultan Ahmed al Mansur Addahbi of the Sa'adian dynasty, and of Queen Elizabeth I.

The following list only mentions the names of the ambassadors and envoys of the Kingdom of Morocco to the United Kingdom; with the specific year of their respective designation, together with the names of the Moroccan and British monarchs or rulers of the time.

The true Effigies of ye Alkaid (or Lord) Jaurar Ben Abdella
Embassador from ye high and mighty Mully Mahamed
Sheque, Emperourr of Morocco, King of Fess and Suss. &c
G. Glover fc.

THE LIST

1   Ambassador Rais Merzouk – (Ahmed Belkacem)[3] – 1588
    Sultan Ahmed el Mansur As-Sa'di / Queen Elizabeth I

2   Ambassador Caid Ahmed ben Adel[4] – 1595
    Sultan Ahmed el Mansur As-Sa'di/ Queen Elizabeth I

3   Ambassador Abdelwahed Benmassaud 'Anoune[5] – 1600
    Sultan Ahmed el Mansur As-Sa'di / Queen Elizabeth I

4   Envoys Mohammed ben Said and Ahmed (Ben Hussein) Narvaez[6] –
        1627
    Mohammed al 'Ayachi, Governor of Sale / King Charles I

5   Envoy Pasha Ahmed ben Abdallah – 1628
    HRH Prince Abdelmalek Benzidane As-Sa'di / King Charles I

6   Envoy Mohammed Clafishou – 1629
    Mohammed al 'Ayachi, Governor of Sale / King Charles I

7   Ambassador Caid Jaudar ben Abdallah[7] – 1637
    Sultan Mohammed Sheikh al Asghar As-Sa'di/ King Charles I

8   Ambassador Caid Mohammed ben Askar[8] – 1638
    Sultan Mohammed Sheikh al Asghar As-Sa'di/ King Charles I

9   Envoy Robert Blake[9] – 1639
    Sultan Mohammed Sheikh al Asghar As-Sa'di / King Charles I

10 Envoy Abdelkrim Annaqsis[10] – 1657
    Ahmed el Haj Dilai (Marabout) / King Charles II

11 Ambassador Mohammed ben Haddu Attar[11] – 1681
    Sultan Moulay Ismail / King Charles II

12 Ambassador Admiral Abdallah ben Aicha[12] – 1685
    Sultan Moulay Ismail / King James II

13 Envoys Mohammed Cardenas and Haj Ali Saban – 1700
    Sultan Moulay Ismail / King William

14 Ambassador Joseph Diaz (between 1700 and 1718, no exact date
    was found)[13]:
    Sultan Moulay Ismail / Queen Anne or George I

15 Ambassador Ahmed ben Ahmed Cardenas – 1706
Sultan Moulay Ismail / Queen Anne

16 Envoy Bentura de Zari[14] – 1710
Sultan Moulay Ismail / Queen Anne

17 Ambassador Abdelkader Perez[15] – 1723
Sultan Moulay Ismail / King George I

18 Ambassador Mohammed BenAli Abghali[16] – 1725
Sultan Moulay Ismail / King George I

19 Ambassador Abdelkrim Benzacor[17] – 1756
Sultan Sidi Mohammed III / King George II

20 Ambassador el Haj Abdelkader Adiel – 1762
Sultan Sidi Mohammed III / King George II

21 Ambassador Admiral el Haj el Arbi ben Abdellah ben Abi Yahia al
Mestiri[18] – 1766
Sultan Sidi Mohammed III / King George II

22 Ambassador Jacob Benider[19] – 1772
Sultan Sidi Mohammed III / King George II

23 Ambassador Sidi Taher ben Abdelhaq Fennish[20] – 1773
Sultan Sidi Mohammed III / King George II

24 Envoy Mas'ud de la Mar[21] – 1781
Sultan Sidi Mohammed III / King George II

25 Ambassador Meir ben Macnin[22] – 1827
Sultan Moulay Abderrahman / King George V

26 Ambassador al Amine Said Mohammed As-Shami[23] – 1860
Sultan Sidi Mohammed IV / Queen Victoria

27 Ambassador Haj Mohammed Zebdi[24] – 1876
Sultan Moulay Hassan I / Queen Victoria

28 Ambassador Mohammed ben Abdallah ben Abdelkrim Assafar[25] –
1880
Sultan Moulay Hassan I / Queen Victoria

29 Ambassador HRH Prince Moulay Mohammed[26] – 1897
Sultan Moulay Abdelaziz / Queen Victoria

30   Ambassador al Mahdi al Mnebhi[27] – 1901
      Sultan Moulay Abdelaziz / King Edward VII

31   Ambassador, Pasha and Caid Abderrahmane ben Abdessadek Errifi[28]
      –   1902
      Sultan Moulay Abdelaziz / King Edward VII

32   Ambassador Tahar ben Al-Amine [29] – 1909
      Sultan Moulay Abdelhafid / King Edward VII

33   Ambassador HH Prince Moulay Hassan Benmehdi[30] – 1957
      King Mohammed V / Queen Elizabeth II

34   Ambassador HRH Princess Lalla Aicha – 1965
      King Hassan II / Queen Elizabeth II

35   Ambassador Mohammed Laghzaoui – 1969
      King Hassan II / Queen Elizabeth II

36   Ambassador Thami Ouazzani – 1971
      King Hassan II / Queen Elizabeth II

37   Ambassador Abdallah Chorfi – 1973
      King Hassan II / Queen Elizabeth II

38   Ambassador Badreddine Senoussi – 1976
      King Hassan II / Queen Elizabeth II

39   Ambassador Abdellatif Filali – 1980
      King Hassan II / Queen Elizabeth II

40   Ambassador Mehdi Benabdejlil – 1981
      King Hassan II / Queen Elizabeth II

41   Ambassador Abdeslam Znined – 1987
      King Hassan II / Queen Elizabeth II

42   Ambassador Khalil Haddaoui – 1991
      King Hassan II / Queen Elizabeth II

43   Ambassador Mohammed Belmahi – 1999
      King Mohammed VI / Queen Elizabeth II

NOTES TO THE LIST

1   Through his envoys of the year 1213, King John (excommunicated by the Pope in 1209) asked for the Moroccan Almohad monarch's political and military support in order to eliminate a rebellious English baronage and to contain a threatened invasion of England by King Philippe Auguste of France. In return for the Moroccan monarch's support, King John 'would voluntarily give up to him himself and his kingdom, and if he pleased would hold it a tributary from him; and that he would also abandon the Christian faith, which he considered false, and would faithfully adhere to the law of Mohammed', i.e. Islam; as stated in the record made by Matthew Paris, the contemporary monkish chronicler of St Albans Abbey (England). See pp. 1–5 of P. G. Rogers's book, mentioned in the attached sources.

2   The two Moroccan diplomats were brought to England in 1551 by Captain Thomas Wyndham in his ship 'The Lion' of London, as cited in Nabil Matar's book: *Turks, Moors and Englishmen*, p. 33 and in P. G. Rogers's book, p. 7 (See sources 3 and 7).

   Captain Wyndham (spelt Windam in other documents) led the first known English voyage to Morocco (Safi), in 1551. This contact established with English traders generated a diplomatic relation thenceforth to continue almost without interruption to modern times.

3   Ambassador Rais Merzouk (1588), otherwise known as Ahmed Belkacem, was also Ambassador to Portugal. In Britain he was accompanied by the English commercial agent Henry Roberts and was received in London by over forty members of the Barbary Company, on 12 January 1589.

   He was nominated Ambassador by Sultan Ahmed al Mansur in November 1588, year of the defeat of the Spanish Armada by England. He consequently brought secret proposals aiming at forging a Moroccan – British alliance against Spain and at installing Dom Antonio on the Portuguese throne.

4   Ambassador Caid Ahmed ben Adel (1595) was accompanied, in England, by two Caids (leaders of the Moroccan corsairs) and a retinue of twenty-five or thirty persons.

5   Ambassador 'Anoune (1600) was from Fes. His name was also spelt as 'Annouri or 'Ancune. He was known in England as 'Hamet Xarife'. His embassy included sixteen persons, all Muslims. He brought with him nine Dutch captives.

   His embassy was lodged in the house of an alderman from the Royal Exchange (London).

   A portrait was painted of 'Anoune, located today at Birmingham University.

   Ambassador 'Anoune handed out to Queen Elizabeth a letter of Sultan Ahmedal Mansur, dated 15 June 1600, by which Morocco proposed a military alliance with England in order to dislodge Spain from the Americas.

   The proposed alliance never did materialise since both monarchs died in 1603.

6   Envoy Mohammed Bensaid (1627) was also known as Mahamet Bemay or Lopez de Zapar, a writer from the village of Hornacheros, in Extremadura (thirty-five kilometres from Merida), Spain.

   Together with Narvaez, they were accompanied by Harrison, the English envoy to Sale. King Charles I wanted to negotiate through them with governor Al 'Ayachi the use of Sale as a base of operations against Spain.

   Envoy Ben Said brought with him one hundred British captives.

7   Ambassador Caid Jaudar ben Abdellah (1637) was a convert of Portuguese origin, and a eunuch (see portrait on page 93). He was also the General Commander of the Sudan army of Morocco. He was the first Muslim given a detailed coverage in the London press. His address in London was at Wood Street near St Lawrence Jewry. English society saw in this ambassador the full flourish of Islam. He brought with him to London 366 British captives (See source 8).

   It seems that one result of Ambassador ben Abdallah's diplomatic efforts was King Charles's December 1637 appointment of the first English consul in Morocco, Giles Penn, a merchant in Tetuan, grandfather of the founder of Pennsylvania (USA). He might have resided as a consul either in Sale or in Tetuan (see source 8).

A portrait of ben Abdellah was painted in England.

Jaudar's name was spelt in England as Jaurar (see source 12) or Juder.

8   Ambassador Caid Mohammed ben Askar (1638) became, in 1645, Ambassador to the Netherlands, assisted by Mr Joseph Pallash, a Moroccan Jew from Mogador.

While in England, little has been achieved by Ben Askar because his arrival coincided with the English king's departure for the north to wage war against the Scots.

9   Robert Blake (1639) was a commercial envoy of Sultan Mohammed Sheikh Assaghir (Saadian dynasty). He originally was an English tradesman operating in Morocco.

10 Envoy Abdelkrim Annaqsis (1657) was governor of Tetuan. One of his ancestors who was also governor of Tetuan, M. Abdelkrim Annaqsis, dealt with the British and corresponded directly with King Charles I. Consequently, Nathaniel Luke, a merchant already residing in Tetuan, got appointed as England's second consul there.

11 Ambassador Benhaddu (1681) was a poet, and an elected member of the British Royal Society; travelled to Oxford and Cambridge. He signed agreements at Whitehall (London). During his mission to Britain, he was accompanied by a Moroccan naval captain, Ahmed Louaqash, as his secretary, and by Caid Mohammed al Hafid.

There were poems written about his sumptuous arrival to Britain, descriptions in private correspondence and diaries, and news reports about the ambassador in the 'London gazette'.

A portrait was painted of Benhaddu, located today at Chiswick House, London.

12 Ambassador Benaicha (1685) became ambassador to Paris from 1698 to 1699. Portraits of Benaicha were painted or drawn.

(13 Ambassador Diaz was also appointed to Portugal by sultan Moulay Ismail where he signed on behalf of Morocco the Lisbon agreement with the King of Portugal. He was later disapproved by the Sultan for his alleged misbehaviour during the times of both his postings in London and Lisbon.

14   Envoy Bentura de Zari (1710) was a merchant and an Armenian Christian. He resided in Dartmouth Street in Westminster. He was originally sent by Sultan Moulay Ismail with only an authorisation to procure deer and various commodities from England. He however acted as if he had a mandate from the Sultan to negotiate as an ambassador with plenary powers. He was held in house arrest by the British as a retaliation for the non-release of English captives in Morocco. He remained posted in London from 1710 to 1713. Only on 2 August 1713 was De Zari received in audience by Queen Anne, at Kensington Palace (London).

15   Ambassador Perez (1723) had another relative named Ali Perez who was ambassador to Paris from 1772 to 1773.

16   Ambassador Abghali (1725) remained in London from 10 August 1725 to July 1726. He had the following embassy staff:

Mohammed Benabdessalam, *secretary*
Essaid Ali Ezaim, *intendant*
Ahmed el Batjvi, *servant*
Abdeslam Shene, *servant*
Mohammed Fartat, *servant*
Ahmed Massud, *servant*
Issa Ezzauri
Mohammed el Arabi, *musician*
Mohammed el Kassri, *musician*
Mohammed el Ainab, *musician*
Hossain Emgar, *garde-robe*
Abdessalam Errhwani, *garde-robe*
Ahmed Essbilir, *garde-robe*
Erraiss Mohammed el Eradi, *cook*
        (died and buried in England, from lung inflammation)
Roussel, *English secretary*
Le Client, *interpreter*
Le Client Samuel
Le Client (friend of Roussel the English secretary)

A portrait of Ambassador Abghali was painted in England, today property of the trustees of the Goodwood collection: oil on canvas

(236.2cm x 145.4cm). See manuscript volumes of court records in the collection of Charles Cottrell-Dormer at Rousham Park, near Oxford.

Ambassador Abghali was notably entrusted with the purchase of gunpowder for Moulay Ismail; and with the request of the Sultan to England for a just treatment for the Moroccan Jews who lived in Gibraltar (see p. 87 of P. G. Rogers's book mentioned in the sources).

17 Ambassador Benzacor (1756) was in fact sent by the then Crown Prince Sidi Mohammed ben Abdallah, based upon a procuration from his father, Sultan Moulay Abdallah.

18 Ambassador al Mestiri (1766), originally from Rabat, was accompanied by Haj Mohammed Ass'idi.

19 Ambassador Jacob Benider (1772) was a Moroccan Jew from Gibraltar; his letters of credence were refused by King George III who rather considered him as one of his subjects. Among his mission's orders from Sultan Sidi Mohammed III, was the purchase of an earth globe, an astrolabe and a telescope.

20 Among Ambassador Fennish's missions was the repair of Moroccan cannons, (1773).

Later, in 1786, Ambassador Fennish signed on behalf of the Sultan of Morocco the famous peace and trade agreement with the USA, together with Thomas Barclay, the US envoy to Morocco.

Ambassador Fennish was from Sale.

21 Envoy de la Mar (1781) was a Moroccan Jew trading in Amsterdam. He delivered a letter from Sultan Sidi Mohammed III to King George III relative to Morocco's expulsion from Tangiers of the British Consul General Logie.

22 Ambassador ben Macnin (1827) was a Moroccan Jew from Mogador. His letters of credence were refused by King George IV.

23 Ambassador as-Shami (1860) was accompanied by al-Amine Haj Abderrahmane al 'Aji, and Tahar Fassi, secretary, and a chronicler of their sojourn in Britain (see source 15).

24 Ambassador Zebdi (1876), from Rabat, was also ambassador to France, Belgium, and Italy.

He was accompanied by Benasser Ghannam (intendant), and Driss J'aidi (secretary), a chronicler of their diplomatic mission to several European countries, including Britain (see source 16).

25 Ambassador Assafar (1880) was originally from Tetuan.

26 Ambassador HRH Prince Moulay Mohammed (1897) was a brother of Sultan Moulay Abdelaziz. He never presented his letters of credence to Queen Victoria because he got ill in France while travelling towards the United Kingdom. He therefore returned back to Morocco.

27 Ambassador al Mnebhi (1901) was Morocco's 'overseas minister ', i.e. foreign secretary. He was accompanied to the United Kingdom by al Amine Haj Abderrahmane Bargach and Caid McLean, a Scot, then head of Morocco's Royal Guard.

28 Ambassador ben Abdessadek Errifi (1902) was accompanied by his secretary al Hussain ben Mohammed al Ghassal.

29 Ambassador Tahar ben Al-amine (1909) was accompanied by Mohammed ben Haj al Arbi Benjelloun and Ahmed Benjelloun Touimi.

30 The ambassadors' exact dates of nomination and of end of mission, during the post-independence era, are as follows:

HH Prince Moulay Hassan Ben Mehdi
    from 1 January 1957 *to* 20 March 1965

HRH Princess Lalla Aicha
    from 20 March 1965 to 1 January 1969

Mohamed Laghzaoui
    from 30 April 1969 *to* 9 February 1971

Thami el Ouazzani
    from 27 September 1971 *to* 21 November 1973

Abdellah Chorfi
    from 21 November 1973 *to* 1 November 1976

Badreddine Snousssi
    from 9 December 1976 *to* 16 April 1980

Abdellatif Filali
from 17 April 1980 *to* 1 March 1981

Mehdi Benabdeljalil
from 5 November 1981 *to* 1 January 1987

Abdessalam Znined
from 16 January 1987 *to* 19 June 1991

Sidi Khalil Haddaoui
from 19 June 1991 *to* 1 September 1999

Mohamed Belmahi from 12 November 1999 —

Source Ministry of Foreign Affairs and Cooperation of Morocco, Rabat

SOURCES

1   د. عبد الهادي التازي : التاريخ الدبلوماسي للمغرب؛ مطابع فضالة -المحمدية. المغرب؛ 1986.

2   د. عـبـد العزيز بنعبد الله : السفارة والسفراء بالمغرب عبر التاريخ ؛ وزارة العدل، المعهد الوطني
     للدراسات القضائية، الرباط؛ 1985.

3   Rogers, P .G., *A History of Anglo-Moroccan Relations to 1900*, Foreign
     and Commonwealth Office, London, UK, 1970s

4   Rogerson, Barnaby, *A Traveller's History of North Africa*, Windrush
     Press, Gloucestershire, UK, 1998

5   St John Parker, Michael, *Britain's Kings and Queens*, Pitkin
     Unichrome Ltd, Andover, Hampshire, UK, 1999.

6   Mackenzie, Donald, *The Khalifate of the West*, London, UK, 1911
     and reprinted by Darf Publishers Ltd, 1987

7   Matar, Nabil, *Turks, Moors and Englishmen in the Age of Discovery*,
     Columbia University Press, New York, 1999

8   Matar, Nabil, *Islam in Britain 1558–1685*, Cambridge, UK, 1998

9   de Castries, Le Compte Henry (editor), *Les Sources Inedites de L'Histoire du Maroc: Archives et Bibliotheques d'Angleterre*, Vol. 1, Editions Ernest Leroux, Paris, 1918; Vol. 2, Geuthner, Paris, 1925

10   de Castries, Le Compte Henry, (editor and translator). *Une Description du Maroc sous le Regne de Moulay Ahmed El-Mansour (1596), d'apres un Manuscrit Portugais de la Bibliotheque Nationale*, Ernest Leroux, Paris, 1909

11   Allin, Thomas, *The Journals of Thomas Allin, 1660–1678*. 2 vols, edited by R. C. Anderson, Navy Records Society, London 1939–40

12   Allin, Thomas: *The Arrivall and Intertainements of the Ambassador, Alkaid Jaurar ben Abdella, with his associate, Mr Robert Blake (1637)*

13   Playfair, Sir R. Lambert and Brown, Dr Robert, *A Bibliography of Morocco from the Earliest Times to the End of 1891*, London, 1892

14   Meakin, Budgett, *The Moorish Empire*, London, 1899

15   الطاهر الفاسي : "الرحلة الإبريزية الى الديار الإنجليزية" كتبت في 1860 ونشرت في 1963. الرباط.

16   إدريس الجعايدي : " إتحاف الأخيار بغرائب الأخبار " (أواخر 1880) . أنظر أطروحة معنينو على تحقيق هذا الكتاب بجامعة محمد الخامس - الرباط - (أواخر 1980).

THE ART DECO OF TUNIS

PETER MORRIS

UNTIL recently, Tunis' (and Tunisia's) colonial architecture has been largely ignored. This is understandable given the historical background, but enough time has now passed for sensitivities to begin to fade, and the colonial legacy is beginning to attract some attention.

Three early examples of the new French rulers trying to stamp the authority of their physical presence on the city are the main Post Office; the Cathedral and French Residence, facing each other across Avenue Bourguiba. On a more mundane level is the vast complex of warehouses below the Jellaz Cemetery with their characteristic walls of pale yellow wash and red tiled roofs. Subsequently, architects succumbed to the fussiness of provincial wedding-cake elaboration (Theatre, ave Bourguiba; 40–42 rue Oum Khalthoum; Hotel Majestic, 36 ave de la Liberte), with occasional forays into 'Moorish' kitsch (9 rue Charles de Gaulle; Villa Timsit, junction of Koweit and Cologne).

By far the most interesting facet of the colonial heritage, though, is the wealth of Art Deco architecture that was built in the period from 1925–40. A 1994 study by an Italian architect identified over four hundred buildings, many of which can still be seen within the grid-plan districts of the modern city: luxurious urban villas, apartment buildings, tenements, office blocks even the main synagogue at 43 ave de la Liberte. Many of the buildings are now somewhat rundown – don't expect another South Beach, Miami – but once you start to pick them out they give the modern city an unexpectedly stylish flavour.

Art Deco burst on the world scene at the Paris Exposition of 1925. Strictly speaking, the term refers more to decorative arts than to architecture as such. But it has come to be applied equally to buildings that feature exuberantly stylised decorations and clean geometric forms.

42 Rue Ibn Khaldoun

20 Rue de L'Inde

On Avenue Hedi Chaer

To architects in colonial North Africa, these characteristics may have made Art Deco seem an appropriate Western successor to inherited local styles, as well as being up with the home country's latest trends. To a contemporary eye their work certainly comes as a welcome breath of fresh air after the ponderous excesses of early colonial work.

The acknowledged masterpiece of Tunis' Art Deco period is the Villa Boublil, a magnificent villa standing near the Belvedere Park at 16 rue d'Autriche. This was built in 1931–2 by an architect called J. G. Ellul, who was born into Tunis' Maltese community in 1890. Even in its current semi-abandoned state, it's well worth a special visit for its rippling lines, which are reminiscent of the 1927–8 Palais de la Mediterranée casino on Nice's Promenade des Anglais. Look out also for the palm-tree motif in the villa's elaborate metalwork. A couple of years later in 1933–5, Ellul also designed an office building (the Omnium Immobilier Tunisien, 12 ave Habib Thameur) whose discreet elegance would not be out of place in a contemporary development. It remains a prestigious address.

Not all the buildings are up to Ellul's standard, and many are routine to the point of blandness. But it's well worth casting your eye above street level every now and then to look out for tell-tale semicircular balconies, crowning Egyptian-style pylons (one of Art Deco's inspirations was the discovery of Tutankhamun's tomb in 1922), elaborate geometric reliefs and above all the metalwork, which appears both on balconies and in doors and windows. Hallway interiors are often elaborately decorated.

Sometimes the effect is on the small scale: a hint of waviness in the metalwork of a balcony. Elsewhere you find a grand statement: three apartment buildings by the same designer filling one whole side of a city block (Q. Riccardini, west side of rue du 18 Janvier 1952 south of rue Ahmed Tlili; P. P. Ancona, north side of rue Ghedhahem east of rue Ibn Khaldoun). If you pass through the Metro station at Place de la Republique, for example, look up to see how the tall towers of the Hotel Ritza (56 ave de Paris, 1929–30) and the Immeuble Zana (2 ave de la Liberte, 1931–3) face each other like ship's prows across the Place. Both are the work of Rene Audineau, born in Tunis in 1904. The architects' names, often visible near the main doorway, offer an informal index of the varying backgrounds of pre-war Tunis' professional classes: Aghilone, Ancona, Audineau, Boccara, Ellul, Raccah, Radicioni, Silvia, Valensi.

The densest concentration of buildings can be found north of ave

Rue des Selines

Habib Bourguiba. For the purposes of the following list (which is not comprehensive), the city centre is divided into four areas; North, Central, South and Monfleury. Montfleury is the colonial suburban district south-west of Bab Aleoua bus station. Particularly fine examples are marked with an asterisk and street junctions are shown in brackets where appropriate

NORTH (north of ave de Londres)

1 rue Abou Doulama (Palestine)

13 rue Ampere (Chedly Kallala)

16 rue d'Autriche* (Ibn Tafragin)

2, 3–5–7 rue du Canada

19 rue du Cap Vert

7, 26, 56, 59 ave Chedly Kallala

1–3, 12* rue d'Egypte

9 rue Ibn Tafragin

20 rue de l'Inde* (Asdrubal)

1 rue Jebel Bargou (Lyon)

10 rue Khartoum

26 rue du Koweit (Asdrubal)

43 rue du Liban (Koweit)

2*, 7, 36, 41, 43* (synagogue), 45*, 61, 79, 105, 131* ave de la Liberte

35, 37, 38bis, 41 ave de Lyon

1*, 2ter, 13, 15, 33 (Hotel Madrid), 46 ave de Madrid

12 rue Menzel Bourguiba

18, 20, 22, 26, 32, 48, 79–81 rue de Palestine

4 Passage no. 1 (Palestine)

9 rue Pierre Curie

5 rue Tatouan

3 rue Tazarka (Lyon)

CENTRAL (ave de Londres to ave Bourguiba)

11 rue Ahmed Bayram

6 rue Annaba

7 rue de la Banque

5 bis rue Gandhi

21, 23, 25, 61 ave Bourguiba

12*, 18 ave Habib Thameur

4, 26 rue Hedi Nouira

1 rue Kamel Ataturk (Bourguiba)

95–97–99, 139 ave de Londres

4, 8 rue Malta Sghira

24, 39 rue de Marseille

8, 10 place de la Monnaie

16, 56* ave de Paris

10 rue de Sparte

SOUTH (south of ave Bourguiba)

8, 11, 29, 40 rue du 18 Janvier 1952

12 rue Ahmed Tlili

22 rue d'Algerie* (Al Jazira)

18 rue Ali Darghouth (Abderrazak Cheraibi)

34*, 48, 59, 62 ave Farhat Hached

47, 71, 77 rue Houcine Bouzaiene

39, 40, 41, 42 rue Ibn Khaldoun

13*, 16 rue Oum Khalthoum

7, 49, 84, 96 rue de Yougoslavie

MONTFLEURY

21 rue Allal El Fassi* (Sadok)

8–10 rue de Moscou

49, 51 ave Taha Hussein (9 Avril 1938)

3 rue Zinelabidine Esnoussi

KING GEORGE V COMES TO MANCHESTER

'ABD AL-MAJID BIN JALLUN, TRANSLATED FROM THE ARABIC BY PETER CLARK

F ROM the 1830s to the 1930s Manchester hosted a Moroccan community that was involved in exporting Lancashire textiles to North Africa. 'Abd al-Majid bin Jallun (1919–81) was the son of one of the merchants and lived with his family in Southern Manchester during the 1920s. He went on to have a distinguished career as nationalist, writer, public servant and diplomat. He wrote his autobiography, *Fi'l-Tufula* (In Childhood) between 1949 and 1952. The following is an extract.

'His Majesty the King of the England and Emperor of India'! Wasn't this a title to excite a child whose imagination was stirred by heroes, fables, celebrities and wielders of sceptres and of power? Was it not the most magnificent, the most glorious and most felicitous of titles? How then could he even utter the name of one on whose possessions and domains in the whole world the sun never set?

Yes, the child began to hear talk of King George the Fifth, Monarch of the United Kingdom and Emperor of India talk that glorified him and magnified him. Whenever he heard talk such as this he imagined that it was about some personage whose majesty and high rank could be neither felt nor seen. The image left in his mind was like that of talk he heard about Almighty God.

What would the your feelings be like if a messenger were to come to you and tell you that God, may His name be held holy was going to pass along the street in which you lived at five o'clock on some particular day? Such feelings would be exactly those that possessed me when I heard that King George V, at the mention of whose names eyes were lowered was going to pass – in person – along that very street in which we lived at five o'clock the day after tomorrow.

I tried to resort to logic in dealing with something I could not comprehend, which happened whenever I came face to face with some new romance.

The people next door started to put up bunting to welcome the great King on his visit to our venerable commercial city, during which he would deign to pass along our humble, oh so humble, street.

The neighbours and people of the area did not just put up bunting. They did everything to enhance the mythical personage's highness and majesty. Bright colours glittered before my mind, and forms and images followed each other in my imagination. First I conjured up the picture of some perfectly formed creature from whose body there gleamed a brilliant light that the human eye could not behold for any length of time. Then I would imagine a mighty powerful giant who would arrive in some fantastic chariot from somewhere between the heavens and earth. Yes, he would come down from the sky above, astride a cloud of light and parade through the street. And the people would be delighted to cast on his gleaming face a glance never to be forgotten.

I could ask someone either from my own household or from the family next door.

But I felt embarrassed at revealing my ignorance about some one about whom it was not proper to be ignorant. I could remember the looks I received when I got round to asking about God and what He looked like, so I would be able to visualise him. And so I preferred to hold back. I would find out the whole truth at five o'clock in the afternoon the following day.

I passed the night, my imagination racing with brilliant images. I could not distinguish between my dreams and my imagination. All the images revolved around the notion of a mighty monarch on whom I would set eyes at five o'clock the following day.

I was always delighted whenever I encountered something new. In that I was like any other child. Each one of us can still remember the feelings that possessed us when we saw this or that for the first time. I woke up next morning, seeing it as the most wonderful day in all my life. My feelings were intensified when I looked out of the window and saw the street decked out as never before in the most brilliant colours.

Here and there in the street there were towering English policemen wearing black uniforms studded with bright brass buttons and gleaming boots. Their legendary composure was wonderful. You would think they had been newly minted just half an hour earlier for this auspicious occasion.

Every now and again a motorbike went by ridden by a police officer who seemed to be part of the machinery.

Incidents followed one another. The hour of the visit approached. The pavement became crowded. All traffic was stopped. Residents and their guests crowded at all the windows and on all the balconies. It was a fantastic sight. I had never seen anything like it before.

My excitement reached boiling point when a guard of honour marched along the street in their glorious uniforms to a band: it was as if I was seeing them at the theatre.

The spectacle then began to move to a more interesting stage. Military units appeared on the street, gloriously dressed, marching to the music, but without any sense of triumphalism.

When I glanced down at the pavements – I was surrounded by a great number of people whom I did not know, the number increasing as the minutes ticked away – it seemed to me that they had disappeared behind thousands of Union Jacks.

I detected an unusual surge coming from the tightly packed crowd, announcing that the anticipated hour was now happily upon us. A thrill soon swept through the crowds, communicating itself to the windows and balconies.

The thrill turned into a strange emotional excitement. People started to cheer and clap and wave their flags. Suddenly I was aware that everyone sitting on the balcony and at the windows were standing up and were sharing all sorts of feelings of wonder.

At this point I was conscious of the fact that the wave of excitement was sweeping me away, and that under its pressure, I could not distinguish one thing from another. I decided to concentrate on gazing at the demigod as he passed along our street and to follow everything that was around me.

I am certain that I did follow everything that was going on in front of me, and can swear that I saw every hand that clapped, every mouth that shouted, every small flag that was waved, and every movement however small in that mass that of people I was looking at. I concentrated with the utmost care such an extent that I did not realise that those with me on the balcony were shouting at me,

'Look, the King, the King!'

I turned round to those shouting at me to check whether they were in their right minds. I then looked where they were pointing and my eye fell on 'the King'! I checked to see whether the person they were pointing at was indeed 'the King''.

Then suddenly some hidden hand wiped the crowds away from the street, like chalk being wiped away from the blackboard. The din died away and the music vanished. It seemed to me that some monstrous fraud had been blown up and up until it had burst.

I left the balcony, disillusioned and angry. I was like a child whose father has promised him a long promised fantastic toy. Then when he receives the toy he finds it is just one of his old toys.

'Did you see the King?' Father asked.

'No.'

'Couldn't you make out the person I was pointing at'?

'Yes, but he was just an ordinary person, not the King.'

Father laughed. Perhaps he realised what was going on inside my mind, which was: His Majesty King George V, Sovereign of the United Kingdom and Emperor of India, has two feet, two hands, a chest and a head, a face, a nose, a mouth and two eyes. You're making fun of me, Daddy. If he's the King, then we are each one of us His Majesty King George V, Sovereign of the United Kingdom and Emperor of India.

'Say anything rather than that, Daddy.'

KEITH DOUGLAS IN NORTH AFRICA
An appreciation by Barry Cole

K EITH DOUGLAS was probably the best English poet of the Second World War: he was also the best war poet since Wilfred Owen in World War One. Owen died at twenty-five; Douglas at twenty-four. And both died in action.

Formally, Douglas learned from Owen and other First World War poets such as Siegfried Sassoon and Robert Graves, who also saw fierce action in battle but managed to live into their eighties.

Like his predecessors, he seemed to master the art and craft of poetry without difficulty. That which he wrote, briefly, before 1939 shows him as a sort of Auden stripped of the intellectualising which dogged the latter in the nineteen-thirties.

Douglas was born in 1920 and, in the manner of his class, educated at public school and at Oxford University, where coincidentally, he was taught by another fine World War One poet, Edmund Blunden. His role in the war was mainly occupied in North Africa, a Maghreb which meant little to the troops fighting there: to them it was simply a battleground upon which they had been placed by fate.

Douglas's attitude towards the war in the desert, towards the enemy – the Germans and, to a lesser extent, the Italians – was one of detachment. He was not a hater of people, and in his remarkable prose book about the desert campaign. *Alamein to Zem Zem*, he can be seen in incident after incident as the objective observer. What makes this record impressive is that it was written, literally, under fire. As must have been at least the ideas for the poems. Wordsworth's suggestion that poetry was emotion recollected in tranquillity just couldn't happen – a tranquil war is oxymoronic in extreme. He was, as a tank commander, fired upon, and shelled. And in his turn, he shot and shelled back. He was also bombed, blown up by mines (he was severely injured by a land-mine), and after a stay in a Cairo hospital, he returned to England to train for the Second Front – the invasion of Europe.

While in England he put together a collection of his poems, to be called 'Bete Noire'. He wrote to his editor: 'I can't afford to wait, because of military engagements which may be the end of me.' This premonition, as Lawrence Durrell called it, was all too real. On his third day in Normandy, on 9 June 1944, Douglas was killed, after getting information from behind the enemy lines. He was twenty-four.

During the North African campaign there were of course other privations at the very least not conducive to the writing of poems: heat, cold, thirst, hunger, sickness, fear. A poignant aspect is that many of these had a place-name attached, which give geographical reality to lines he wrote. Twenty years after the war, his *Collected Poems* appeared, and a new edition of *Alamein to Zem Zem. Selected Poems*, edited by the late poet laureate, Ted Hughes, appeared in 1964. In his introduction, Hughes wrote:

> The war brought his gift to maturity, or to a first maturity. In a sense, war was his ideal subject: the burning away of all human pretensions in the ray cast by death. This was the vision, the unifying generalisation that shed the meaning and urgency into all his observations and particulars: not truth is beauty only, but truth kills everybody.

He sums up: [His poetry] is a language of and for the whole mind at its most wakeful, and in all situations. A utility general-purpose style as, for instance, Shakespeare's was, that combines a colloquial readiness with poetic breadth . . . In the end, an achievement for which we can be grateful.'

THE BUTCHER'S AESTHETICS

MOHAMED MAGANI

An extract translated by Lulu Norman

I

THE surname Chafra Elgataâ[1] stuck with me long after I left Lattifia.
Although the butcher's shop was sold to my neighbour the carton-of-red-wine-butcher for next to nothing, with my mother into the bargain, I
dragged it around like a birthmark, a whim of nature that passing time did
nothing to erase from people's memories. When I returned to the village I
was invariably greeted with 'Hi there, Chafra' 'Echafra's back', 'Where've
you been, Echafra?' I didn't mind being called by a surname linked to my
profession *before* the event that made me leave Lattifia, but *after*, years
after, to tell the truth I could not help wondering what people might be
thinking. I would repeat the same line with everyone I met: 'You are
mistaken. I have killed no one, my brothers, it wasn't me.'

The semi-solitude that was forced upon me, the falsely polite
silences, the sideways looks, the whispering that lacerated my back, the
underwater way people behaved, everything in slow motion (born of
nonchalance, idleness or simply the boredom of village life), put me off
the idea of opening a new butcher's, wanting to spare my children the
consequences of a slander whose effects they could gauge amongst their
school friends in the street, and almost always in the bosom of the family.
My wife, bless her, had no doubts about my innocence, and would give
the sharp end of her tongue to those who were obsessed with the idea of
the murderous butcher (though seldom in my presence), the people of
Bled Ya Latif [2] – her cutting distortion of Lattifia – who had had it in for
me ever since one of the large knives from my shop was discovered near
the mayor's corpse.

1 *el gataâ*   Arabic meaning the cleaver, cutter, slicer
2 *Bled Ya Latif*   wordplay on Lattifia, meaning 'godforsaken place'

How the knife disappeared from the butcher's remained a mystery for years, until the day I again met the man who had irrefutably established my innocence before the Lasnam judges: the Lattifia chief of police. A remarkable man, blessed by heaven with a gift for boundless friendship, whose only link with power was reduced to a few bits of sea-green fabric, the uniform he wore as no soldier has ever worn the garb of power – he floated inside it like a body in space. God who created time created it in sufficient quantity for two people at least to get to know each other, whose intuition of myriad events established a link beyond the usual limits imposed by the minefield of personal relationships. The other gendarmes would call me by my surname, but from our very first meeting he asked me my first name, the real one, without ever mentioning the surname, except for once when he wrote to me from his remote village in the Oran area, his letter beginning with a 'Dear Ech . . . ' swiftly concealed under two immaculate blots of black, like two perfect squares on a draughts board, a substantial slip of the pen visible on the other side of the paper. The letter arrived a month after he left Lattifia forever, happy to put an end to the long unbroken years at his post. His absence revived the shady, mafioso dealings of the gendarmes who lived off the backs of butchers, grocers, greengrocers, shoemakers – the list could run to practically all businesses. No one in Lattifia could accuse him of having encouraged those rackets. It should be said, too, that the retailers and wholesalers had themselves begun to bribe the gendarmes as soon as they had settled in the village, for example some butchers would send their wives quarters of meat, delivered by idle children who hung around the streets.

In those days, in the long years of post-independence, the resistance fighters who came back from the mountains or from abroad were given a heroes' welcome, and very soon became super-citizens of undisputed moral authority, especially in the villages. We didn't yet have a police station (policemen appeared after the first four-storey buildings were built); the gendarmes were our first experience of the new regime. I too had given in to their sporadic demands. When they had no intention of paying, they would usually send a child, who repeated the eternal order: 'My father would like two pounds of meat', sometimes four pounds, rarely more; if the request exceeded six pounds the child would reappear several weeks later. At dawn one morning I made a resolution to refuse to comply with the orders conveyed by the children, the day I witnessed an intimidation in the shop of the only Tunisian in the village.

This man was known to all the families, he would come back to Lattifia every year before the month of Ramadan to resume his business, which was baking fried sugar pastries and doughnuts, the particular, indispensable ingredient of the meals that reverse the succession of day and night. As far back as I can remember, from my childhood until the event that hurried the departure of the unfortunate pastry-seller that year, I had had a pronounced weak spot for plain doughnuts. My first daily ritual, before opening the door to the butcher's, was to have four or six of them with two cups of tea, to which I would add a bunch of mint. I would eat the doughnuts quickly, wasting no time over my first cup, waiting for the second to sip slowly and begin the conversation that would finally rouse me from the night's sleep.

That day I had lingered in the pastry shop because the weekly market where I sometimes sold meat was too far from Lattifia and not worth the journey. I'd only just started to leave when a familiar figure barred my way. I stopped dead. The gendarme known in the village as the 'Whale' planted himself in the doorway. A colossal body, powerful arms and legs, his enormous belly half-covered by a ridiculously short pyjama top, he stood still for an electric moment. A threatening arm was raised, a tornado of insults flew from the mouth of the gendarme who stood facing me, before he turned suddenly to the pastry-seller and said: 'You Tunisian bastard! You won't last long here, I guarantee it!'

'But . . . ' the pastry-seller protested tersely.

'I'll pay you for your blasted doughnuts!' the gendarme shouted. 'Don't send my son back to me empty-handed again!'

He turned on his heel, threatened the floor with his fist and left. The Tunisian gazed wearily at the walls of his shop and the pyramids of pastries on the trays around him, and let himself flop onto a chair. 'It happens to us all,' he said. He knew the sacrifices I made to provide the free meat, but until then we had not discussed our cowardice. It was that day, dear reader, my brother and sister, that my decision was taken: the tools of my trade, however sharp, would no longer cut meat for super-citizens. I imagined the worst: the butcher's closing, trumped-up charges, every kind of harassment, judicial proceedings, physical intimidation, verbal threats, prison, a compromise solution with other butchers or local officials acting as go-betweens. The idea of a boycott crossed my mind too, without my decision being altered: I would not back down, nor take orders from children. I never found out whether these sanctions would have been taken, the diminutive emissaries never put me to the test, for the week after the pastry-seller had been brought to book, a man arrived in the village who would transform the relationship between the gendarmes and the shopkeepers forever.

My first encounter with the new chief of police of the gendarmerie took place in the butcher's one evening as I was putting away sheep's heads and legs that were laid out on a long, short-legged table, carefully covered with small branches of eucalyptus. The man was walking with his head down, as if the peak of his helmet indicated the place on the ground that his eyes scrutinised so relentlessly, mysterious fragments placed on thin strips of glass for microscopic observations. This was how, he told me later, once our meetings had lost something of the proprieties of chief of police/customer on his side and zealous butcher on mine, he had missed so few films in his far-off village near Oran. The price of entry to the cinema was one dinar going up to one dinar fifty, the rise denoting the beginning of a ticket system, a sum neither his father nor mother could afford to give him every Friday night. So his strategy lay in going round the village staring at the ground: the number of coins that gleamed or lay hidden under a thin layer of dust would come to far more than the cost of entry, provided he set about it straight after the films ended and went on until the week was up. He would usually pick up at least enough for three seats, which his friends would then fight over. Those films were his ticket to the world.

The doughnut incident was no doubt not insignificant in paving the way for a long friendship between myself and the chief of police. The state of mind in which I found myself, a boiling rage mixed with a deep sense of failure, and from time to time the optimistic calm of renewed resolution, made all my thoughts turn to the imagined possession of a machine gun, a recoilless rifle or a sword (preferably the same as Khaled's [3]) and injected a strong dose of aggression into my words. So his first visit to the butcher's coincided with a long period of inner turmoil, manifest in

---

3 *Khaled* companion of the prophet Mohammed, often depicted with an ornate sword.

my constant finger-cracking, which those close to me remarked on. The nervousness with which I cut the meat on the block, the violent slamming of the cold store door, and the cutlets which, in my hurry, slid off the scales and fell to the floor at my feet, culminated in the dry, openly hostile, almost contemptuous phrase: 'That will be twenty-one dinars'.

I still remember his words – calm, distant, free of animosity, with just a hint of irony: 'How kind,' he said, poker-faced. 'I pay for my purchases in cash. It's one of my principles. My name is Sayad, I think we'll be friends. From today, I'll be one of your most regular customers.' It was as if he'd operated to open my brain and emptied my head of all its black thoughts, drawn from my body all the fury that had drained my energy, uselessly – dead meat.

I had no time to answer. He left the butcher's staring down at his feet and did not look back. I stood there, perplexed, the money still in my hand, realising the extent of my blunder, the misunderstanding caused by my stubbornness. Happily, I never had the chance to prostrate myself in sorrow and regret, for the simple reason that at our second meeting, which took place in the Gendarmerie itself, he was very sympathetic and soon cut short my attempts at self-justification by explaining that in this kind of situation it was difficult to lay the blame on one party. It was still early days for our country, he said, and unfair to ally oneself with one protagonist, one party, one tendency, without jeopardising the future, since we lacked materials, a past, beaten pathways and proofs: when the sun comes out, what shines is just a thin film of dust. In the future, responsibility would be shared.

I had been sitting opposite him listening, because he had moved his chair behind his desk, trying to grasp the meaning of his words, words I would remind him of long after he'd left the village for good, for Oran, the city he settled on both to launch his three driving schools and to be near his sick mother.

It was summer. Early in the morning I would slip silently out of the house where my mother, my wife and children were still sleeping, and have my usual breakfast of doughnuts and tea with my friend the Tunisian, who was no longer worried about relations with the gendarmes, thanks to the vigilance of the new chief of police – Sayad showed exemplary firmness toward his men in uniform. Then I would head for the butcher's, which I did not leave until evening. An hour after waking, my late father used to swallow a few figs soaked in olive oil, from a jealously guarded bottle kept under the block. He would clean his work tools, wipe down furniture and walls with a damp sponge, open the shop door, then conscientiously take from the cold store quarters of meat, heads, legs and offal which he would hang on the hooks, display on the low table outside or throw into the basin. It was a pleasant enough occupation in the coolness of the morning, but the long hot hours of summer that followed were meagre in customers. He would await them until dusk, never leaving the butcher's even for a minute, and would pray there in the furnace of the afternoon, a dead time in the village.

Summer afternoons were the beginning of my hardly gainful initiation into the butcher's trade, begun as a child. In spite of his protestations when I laughed at his waning energy, my father had aged appreciably in the warm months, when he would spend longer praying and taking his siesta. He was halving the time he spent in the shop, which he deserted at lunchtime and returned to in the evening, just before closing. Then it was my turn to wait for the phantom customers.

Unable to resist the drowsiness that would invade my mind, engulfed in the fatal brightness of those hours of lemony light so lethal for business, sitting on my chair I would make imaginary efforts to prevent my head nodding and keep my eyes open, but would sink into the fog of drowsiness and finally doze off with my head between my arms spread out on the block, defeated by the shadowy light, tired of watching the entrance to the shop – a useless precaution when I knew that even our animal clientele was not interested in meat at that ungodly hour. It was these moments of relaxation that my father would choose to suddenly reappear, sometimes with no noise, his tall, unreal, floating silhouette filling the doorway, creating for a moment a dense, mobile shadow theatre, almost a slow motion native dance, whose effect, far from shaking me out of my torpor, intensified my body's collapse into a lethargy that verged on general anaesthesia. He would never jerk me awake with violent gestures or shouting; my father would not move from his spot but utter the same words, repeated time and time again in the same bewitching voice, respectful of my sleep, yet heavy with an overwhelming insinuation of fatalism: 'May God rest your soul, but keep you alive'.

I would wake with a start from lay stupor, spring to my feet like a soldier and take hold of his hand which I kissed, my face red with confusion, stammering 'Good afternoon, Sidi'.'. My father, the old fox, used this method several times and almost succeeded in ridding me of my desire to doze during the siesta. So as to stop my eyelids drooping, I would make sure my body was occupied one way or another, whether replacing eucalyptus branches with new ones which I sprinkled with water, or (my favourite pastime, which I endlessly prolonged) cutting my toenails with a knife. It was not enough. My feeble lethargy lost its hold over me once and for all, thanks to two neighbours who began to frequent the shop after the death of my father, whose continuous presence on the premises had been an obstacle to them since primary school. In fact they were more than neighbours, they were friends and brothers, two members of a trio that helped me pass the empty hours of a period both open and closed, a crushing time for generations of people, who had been confined for so long inside mental limitations, reservations for subhuman species, opened up to argument.

I was young and vulnerable, the heir to a butcher's shop, with only a crude understanding of the ways of the world, with no school experience in my family, apart from primary school level among the other kids, with the added responsibility of looking after my mother, who, the moment I turned adolescent, married me to the daughter of a colleague afflicted with the disease of Lattifia's butchers: an unbreakable allegiance to red wine. Arratt, Kaici and later Sayad added to this life doomed in advance to premature conformity, with no alternative roles than duty and servitude to family tradition, a wealth of emotion, reacting to this time come from nowhere, where, perhaps as never before, city and village were in tune. For me, dear reader, my brother and sister, this wealth of emotion meant an active citizenship, a race without winners or losers, an historic overlapping of individual and society – and not just the damaging upsurge of frenzied feeling, but, most of all, passion as the corollary of knowledge, the conviction that we belonged to a greater community forced to rewrite its own prehistory, its history, and the myths that needed inventing in its name. A terrible gordian knot was suffocating our imagination: Arratt, Kaici and Sayad were aware of this, and with their help I was beginning to learn.

Collective experience and a deep desire for knowledge were, I think, the features of the time (how many times had my friends not ridiculed all the people in the village who affixed as many pens to their outside jacket pockets as these could possibly hold). Arratt, Kaici and Sayad had been through all the emotion of their time: generosity, tenderness, irony, a certain propensity for sensual pleasure, the absence of mysteries, and they didn't make any up. They would hide something else, secrets – a secret is not a mystery, it is not to be fathomed, or only rarely. It is hard to learn it; often you don't even know it yourself.

A week was all my mother needed to return to reality after my father's death. On the eighth day she called me into the kitchen where she was cooking white haricot beans without meat, which she would sprinkle with a little liquid harissa – a dish that had often united her, my father and myself around a large, deep plate, steaming with a spicy, slightly copper-coloured sauce – and apprised me of my new responsibilities as head of our little business venture and of the family. Then she immediately sent me on a crash course in the gutting, dismemberment, carving and quartering of meat from lamb and oxen whose throats had been slit by my future father-in-law, the carton-of-red-wine-butcher. She was very strict on the matter of throat-slitting: I was not to be initiated into that art at my tender age. I was to buy the animals and hand them over to the professional throat-slitters who would buckle down to their task early each morning in the abattoir I could just make out from my bedroom window, a building with walls that had eventually assumed the colour of the excrement of the poor creatures killed there. It was windowless, half-hidden by a clump of blackberry bushes at the corner of the vast village souk, surrounded by walls which also took in a football ground left by the enemy soldiers.

My future was sealed by the key to the butcher's shop; as my mother handed it to me she reminded me that from now on she had only God and me. I think at that moment I thought intensely of God, of the abattoir, and of the cemetery at the edge of the village behind the house where I lived: my father had preferred to be buried in another cemetery, far from the village, on a green hill overrun with weeds and scrub all year round – like a final jump, a last-minute escape from a heartbreaking neighbourhood, tomb of so many hopes and dreams. As well as the butcher's I had also taken possession of a place as strange and frightening as the areas of Lattifia where I'd never set foot, on the prison road, at the exact boundary set by the colonists between their houses and the rest, in the vicinity of the brickyard, behind which scoop chains dug clayey earth from the deep crevasse in the centre of the village.

We called it El Forn; my father thought differently, for him it was El Fana.[4] If I opened the window, a breeze came in. If I opened the door it was only to go in or out of my room, the two stone benches on either side were not to my mind a good place for sipping tea or a proper chat, like most doorways, since they faced the yard door which opened straight onto the cemetery. My wife went on and on about the window which I kept shut in summer as in winter, especially in summer when opening the door and window could create a current of fresh air – which my mother also prayed for.

I had passed through my place of birth like a traveller passing through a big city station, a nowhere place, my memories even deny its existence. I read. I read to forget my pain, time, and the school that tormented my nights. I thought of Arratt, Kaici and the other children in the classroom, receiving what seemed to me at the time to be the highest of blessings. Sentence by sentence, page by page, I would speak the words of the only three books my father bought during my primary school years: an arithmetic book, a reading book, and a third full of recitations. Then I would pass to the second stage: books closed, I would laboriously copy the sentences into an exercise book with cross-ruled paper, guided by the music of the pronunciation that lingered in my head. Late in the evening, my mother, alerted by the thread of light from the candle which showed under my door, would call out to me softly, reminding me of her fears before independence any light drew soldiers like honey draws flies – and of the shop where I had to be very early each morning. Curbing my annoyance, I would put out the candle and slide under the covers without stopping my school work. I mentally revised the sentences I'd read for imaginary essays.

This nocturnal homework lasted for months; my mother's pained reproaches contained more and more reprimands, sorrow and anxiety, marking my first terrified sleepless nights in a childhood entirely dominated by my nostalgia for school. It was not the screech of jeeps at night, nor the heavy pacing of soldiers on patrol that caused this terror, but an

4 *el forn* meaning furnace; *el fana* meaning extinction

obsession that I would suddenly be struck blind, lose my sight during the night, never return to school or even to the butcher's. I would jump out of bed and grope for the closed window, inspecting the lower part with my fingers, searching for a ray of light, as if trying to hold in my hands what was by nature intangible. In summer, when peace reigned, I would stretch myself out on the floor and contemplate the stars, trying to count them in imaginary circles, reassured by the flickering light my eyes could see in the dark.

My mother understood the reason for my obstinate insistence on reading late into the night one evening before an Eid[5] when she decided to buy me my first suit (a purchase that would have made my late father very happy, she assured me). We had stopped in front of the only shop window in the village. I was intrigued by an unusual object in the midst of the trousers, shirts, fezes, shoes, handkerchiefs, socks, jackets, braces, buttons, overcoats, burnouses,[6] boxes of firecrackers, a jumble of fabrics . . . There, lying on the shelf, was a small black satchel. Its presence awakened memories of my night-time anguish, and of another event that was common in my childhood: satchel in hand, I would be on the way to school, to find my path blocked by soldiers and their vehicles. Men in uniform shouted at us to go back home and not hang around outside. School was closed, they said, with no explanation. With my friends I would jump for joy, but inside the sadness made its lasting impact, and I would go back home while the others overran the football ground by the souq. In my room a strange need to make a minute inventory of my satchel took hold of me each time, and with the help of pencil, slate and exercise book I would construct the walls of my school, a therapeutic pastime which made my parents feel as gloomy as I did. My mother asked me if there was something I liked in the shop window, and getting no answer she touched my shoulder and looked me straight in the eye.

'Satchel' I blurted, without hesitation. An indescribable pain clouded her face, I saw a veil of tears eclipse her beautiful, chestnut-coloured, almond eyes. 'Come, my son, come,' she said, and we left the window display for the next shop. My mother's attitude changed and she tolerated my night reading after the day we saw that satchel in amongst

5 *Eid* religious festival
6 *burnous* man's over-cloak

the clothes, which she would surely have bought for me had it not been my duty to take care of her; I was already an adult.

She showed no anger or disappointment when my future father-in-law, using his wife as messenger, informed her of Arratt and Kaici's daily presence in the butcher's during the summer holidays of their first year at the Oued Fodda school, visits that none the less stood out owing to the small number of adolescents, out of the mass of illiterates, who studied at the only secondary school in the region during the last year of colonial occupation. The carton-of-red-wine-butcher had insisted, sending his wife on several occasions to persuade my mother to forbid me to see my friends again; according to him, my casual attitude and scorn for what people said constituted a real threat to meat sales. My mother was steadfast in her indulgence that summer and the following summers, once I had reassured her of Kaici and Arratt's intentions; my future father-in-law could not comprehend that the aim of our endless discussions was not to make the business go under – a rumour he had fabricated I suspected, so he might take over the property of a widow and her only child.

The country had been born; now its inhabitants had to be created. This was a superhuman task and one fatally turned toward the past, which revealed itself in scraps, wrenches, painful incisions, always subject to the theoretical guillotine of an intoxicating present, a spiral of convictions which gradually, despite the awareness which was now becoming self-aware, raised monstrous, infinite and intolerable illusions. For a short time, a handful of men and women had believed they possessed what had been lacking for centuries: thought and power, pretending not to know that it was precisely their sterile union that lay behind this age-old waste, a cowardly decline, a fundamental forgetfulness which still haunts the present: the elite of power and knowledge, each complementing the other – a shadow congratulating a shadow. Because of their thirst for knowledge, their forgetting or claiming to forget the village, their ambition to create another at the edge of the first, Arratt, Kaici and later Sayad will always remain exemplary human beings for me, the only ones able to decipher of the details of the immense, metal-spun spider's web in Lattifia, which had frozen time in favour of countless Gods.

The year I became the overnight owner of a butcher's, Arratt and Kaici began to study at the college in Oued Fodda, a village near Lattifia, remarkable for the number of girls in its streets, a feature unrivalled in our own, where they were simply absent. Oued Fodda's luck was due to the college, reopened after independence and near to the larger town of Lasnam, which already had traditional mixed-sex secondary school education. Arratt and Kaici were envious of their friends who lived in Oued Fodda and grumbled about Lattifia's lack of girls.

My friends would come to the butcher's every evening, to report back and try to explain to me what they were learning. Every so often, if I persisted in my ignorance and could not follow their explanations, the two schoolboys would look at each other and roll their eyes. Kaici was the more patient; Arratt would fidget on his chair, irritated by my bovine expression (I often thought the frequent comparisons he made between my face and that of an ox, cow, goat, bull, sometimes a mule, was simply a disarming ploy to discourage me from learning) but I would stand firm and tell them I had no intention of remaining a butcher all my life, before launching into a list of butchers' rights to lodging, a car, freedom of speech, religion and association, and, naturally, the inalienable right to an education. Next I would attack them head-on, calling them arrogant, ungrateful, privileged snobs, with no respect for anyone not as lucky as them, ending with the threat to find other tutors. My attack caused them to fall silent, with a kind of ironic attentiveness. A few collusive seconds would pass, ending with a burst of laughter and a rallying cry: 'Long live butchers!' That voluntary commitment and unshakeable solidarity broke out so many times in the butcher's shop.

In the first year, every subject was on offer: mathematics, history, geography, literature, natural science (I had bought the books they were using and was making steady progress through the syllabus). I would work on them in decreasing order of complexity in my room, with no interruptions from my mother, who was astonished at the temple of knowledge being set up in her house. Arratt and Kaici had their preferences; without knowing it I was hot on their heels. I dropped natural science. Mathematics – particularly geometry, with its lines that the given problem set intertwining, triangulating, describing circles and forming squares – would wipe from my mind the house, the butcher's, the abattoir, the cemetery and the carton-of-red-wine-butcher's muffled threats, and for a few hours late in the night I would imagine myself an architect at work – in those moments the image was so vivid – at the foot of a colossal pyramid commissioned by a pharaoh who was utterly confident in his master builders' skills. Solving a difficult problem would sweep me to instant victorious delight and make my limbs tingle with nervous excitement. I would immediately turn out the light, tune in to the hoarse, caressing, insinuating voices of one of the late-night women broadcasters, and start to masturbate, slowly at first, then frantically, in the erotic half-light created by the rays from the illuminated rectangle in the radio on my chest, until I came in a jet of burning sperm.

Kaici and Arratt also introduced me to a subject which has not yet found its place in school curricula: Bedouin music, my first musical passion. The slow rhythmic simplicity of its regular tempo beats time to silence, madness and wisdom, grace and disgrace, prayer and blasphemy – and more than makes up for them with the fertility of a poetic genre nourished by lyrical shades and counter shades, metaphorical shimmerings that left my friends and me intensely curious, longing to see the lyrics' hidden face. Listening to records and tapes years later convinced me of one thing: the bedouin calls for depths that only a lifetime of exclusion can provide; you have to be old to sing only with words, just the way it is with the blues. I used to keep old records by stars now long gone which made their voices sound distant, as if they were singing without an audience, forsaken, lost on endless plains, guided by a single aim: to restore to life an absent people, in utterly elliptical, almost inscrutable songs. I collected records by the young stars and would travel to hear them, if they performed somewhere near Lattifia. I still remember the evenings in crowded village cafés, with people sitting on chairs or on the ground, motionless, listening to Elattafi imploring tears to end his days – ['Let me weep for the brown-haired girl'] – was a favourite song of my teenage years. The death of the tradition of poetry evenings after one particular springtime, along with the tradition of the meddah[7] and the snake charmers, was, I believe, one of the early warning signs of the tragic manipulation of needs that took out so much energy in a young country. No less tragic was the arrival of the omniscient ethic of consumerism, and the refusal to think in historical terms.

---

7 *meddah*   public story teller

Around this time, the first covered market went up in the centre of the village, a massive building, rising and rising, like the minaret of the mosque. The disappearance of the poetry evenings led to my getting totally absorbed by two subjects Arratt and Kaici continually brought back, bit by bit yet urgently, for they were my passions and theirs: history and literature. Mathematics was getting more and more difficult, geography and natural science lost their appeal when my friends began to complain of the long boring time needed to revise for the exams. I bought my first dictionary. My friends were no longer around to explain the mysteries of language; having completed the second year at Oued Fodda, they continued their studies in Lasnam as boarders at the college there They would return at weekends, take up residence in the butcher's shop and hold forth on their beloved subjects: literature came first, followed by history, which stopped the mind from straying by equipping it with a solid, nomadic, travelling platform.

My mother, who had never seen a dictionary in her life, compared it to the head of a bull without ears, a zelif,[8] and reproached me for keeping her in the dark about my trip to Lasnam, which was motivated by the dictionary and not the Sheherazadesque pretext I had invented, namely applying for a permit from an authority of the wilaya[9] to supply meat to the newly enlarged prison in Lattifia. I answered – another lie – that it was better to buy books than spend the money getting drunk. My mother had nodded, looked at the massive volume for a long while, then smiled, picked it up and placed it on the work table in my room.

The dictionary was my gateway to literature: the words took on the shapes of faces, became people I knew, friends I recognised a long way off. I would read their definitions, copy them into an exercise book, close the book and write them down again on loose sheets of paper which I would throw into the waste paper bin should my memory betray me or meanings get mixed up; sometimes I managed to find several meanings to just one word. With the thick volume out of reach, on a table in my room I forced myself to do the same exercises in my spare moments at the butcher's, recopying the words from the night before, following by a

8 *zelif* cloven hoof
9 *wilaya* department controlling administrative, political and religious affairs of particular region

colon, then writing out their definitions again, on wrapping paper, transforming the big sheets into real hieroglyphic manuscripts. As the months went by I tamed a lot of words, particularly the sweet-sounding ones, whether short or long, and would anticipate their coming, feel their presence on the pages of the first books given me by Kaici and Arratt, the first short stories that would fill me with joy if I could close them without stumbling on one sentence or consulting the dictionary lying beside me on the table, the block or the bed. Literature did not have the same effect on me as mathematics, there were no solutions to be sought, or fear that the light would attract enemy soldiers (they had returned, defeated, to their country). The pleasures of problem-solving and reading were very different, the first was transient, a cold ejaculation, but the second was an intense experience, a ceremonial dance in which I was juggling with the words. I read everywhere, and anything I could lay my hands on: newspapers, comics, affordable books, letters written to illiterate people. Sometimes, not without a certain fear, I would open the amulets my mother had stored up since her marriage, for herself, my late father, and later for my welfare on earth.

Today, years since literature deserted my existence, I often wonder why the novel eventually tired me out, became pointless, an alcoholic's vomitorium, and I instantly remember the anguish that knotted my throat after Sayad's revelation, a serious attack on the time we were living in. 'You are blind,' he had said, in the cave where we often met – him Arratt, Kaici and me – not far from the village, 'The state lacks imagination: it *begins* by building prisons and police stations. Look around you!' The truth came out of his mouth – that was the strong impression he made on me – him, the chief of police of Lattifia. I gave up reading. Selling meat and escaping with my friends determined my life for a long while. I was haunted, too, by the terrible event that occurred between the cave and the village: the assassination of the mayor, and the accusation hanging over me. In my mind, the walls of the prison had never seemed so tangible.

The long summer holidays changed the rhythm of Kaici and Arratt's visits; they would leave Lasnam for more than two months and come back to the butcher's to kill time. They would arrive at siesta time; the heat drove people between walls, and my stepfather would disappear with them. Then we gave free rein to our common passion. Truth became fluid in those empty hours. The mid-afternoon would turn the daylight saffron with an orangy dust, thick and heavy, immobilising life inside the butchery in a series of snapshots. Real life would spring up on all sides, we would slide it open and shut like those thin partitions in Japanese houses, revealing whole sections of our history and everyday life unknown to the village. The litres of water from the big saucepans and the bucket I kept in the cold store fought off our fits of drowsiness or quenched our thirst; with quick ablutions we would counter the effects of the dry, hot atmosphere on our faces, arms, legs and feet. Arratt used to drink a great deal; likewise he would later succumb to a different atmosphere in the cave and sink incredible amounts beer and wine. (A few years later, in his mystical religious phase, far from the temptations of this earthly world, natural sparkling water was the only drink he would accept.) He was also the one who had the most trouble slipping out of the house at times of general disobedience in the village, when a lot of young people would ignore warnings of the risk of sunburn and drowning, escape their watchful parents and run to bathe in the river which had hollowed a bed that curved past the village. Barely thirty yards separated the souq walls from the river bank, a space occupied moreover by a popular springtime attraction: a stud farm which offered the sight of mares coupling, brought out to be covered by stallions.

Of the three of us, Kaici and I suffered the least from paternal constraint, for the simple reason that our fathers were dead. Arratt's father, a saddler, was extremely polite and courteous; rarely seen in the village, he knew but one thing, work. This man seemed to have traced his destiny along a single never-deserted path, a straight line between his workshop and his home. He had always intrigued me as he passed in front of the butcher's, his head bowed in greeting, draped in a white satiny burnous. What was strange was the terror he inspired in his oversized family: his seven children obeyed him slavishly and Arratt carried filial respect to unique extremes: if his brothers and sisters kissed the palm of their father's hand, he would kiss the palm and then the back of his hand several times, and often both hands, as if wishing to hide his face, a ritual observed rigorously throughout all the phases, long or short, of his adherence to religious, mystical or political causes, which all aimed to convert people to -isms, something he was responsible for introducing to the village.

It was one of his ramadanesque moments – that is, one favouring deep thought, more work and even greater self-denial – that Sayad chose for our second meeting. He sent the local official bearing a summons in due form, signed by his own hand. Arratt and Kaici saw the messenger brandishing a rectangular sheet of paper whose contents they did not suspect. The local official handed Arratt the summons and asked him to read it aloud. I was already excluded from the circle of those initiated into the alphabet, typically for butchers and almost all shopkeepers who were accustomed to handling ten figures, not to writing sentences or reading them. Arratt, on the other hand, enjoyed the esteem of a universal scribe; almost every disagreement in which language was central became for him a vocation very early in life, which is even now unrivalled in the village: shades of legal meaning, requests, complaints, administrative correspondence, letters between relatives, friends, lovers, crosswords, Scrabble and local journalism. His appreciation of Sayad's letter confirmed for me his reputation as a first class public writer, a genuine expert in writing:

This man didn't just come down from the mountains,' he said. 'No gendarme in Lattifia could write like this.'

'Yes,' said Kaici, 'it's elegant handwriting. Flawless.'

In the office of the chief of the gendarmerie, I began to understand my friends' opinions. Sayad was young. He would not have been able to bear arms in the mountains. I had thought him about twenty years old, give or take a year or two. I agreed with my friends: he must then have had the opportunity to study. When the gendarme opened the door to his chief's office, he was standing with his back turned to a half-closed metal cabinet, a short-sleeved shirt clinging to skinny, almost hairless arms, and a smile stretching the soft down beneath his nose, making it thinner still 'Ah! Our suspicious butcher!' he said, 'I haven't yet used my uniform to shop with. Perhaps one day I'll organise some crime in your charming village. A racket, what do you say?' His smile was now openly ironic. I protested silently, gesticulating like a dumb man doing penance. 'It's not your fault. I understand the situation.' He sat down behind his desk and gestured to me not to worry. I had not opened my mouth when he took two familiar bottles of Pils from his desk and put one in front of me. Dismayed, feeling more and more uneasy, I stayed where I was, incapable of moving towards the chair.

'Sit down, sit down. I find it very hard to hold frank conversations with perpendicular drinkers. The beer's cold and there are plenty more cans to help pass this blistering afternoon, two hands' worth of fingers.' Raising his right hand, he multiplied the number five several times. 'Believe me, small-time racketeering in villages like Lattifia is nothing new to us. I resist that kind of influence and relationship as far as I can. I grew up in a family of thieves, what I mean is my father is a thief. Coffee, sugar, semolina, oil, and a whole load of other stuff, he gets them for free. He's night-watchman with a wholesaler. The long lonely nights put ideas in his head and he developed an effective technique, which was to make a hole the size of a needle head in the hundred-pound sacks, my father, the dirty crook! He presses all round the holes, and the sugar, coffee, semolina flow out like milk from a cow. Two pounds from each sack! Just enough not to arouse suspicion. Very efficient. He plugs the holes with a grain of wheat or some chewing gum, and hey presto! What do you think of that! My father has ideas for scams galore. I'm telling you because I've seen him at it; it was my job to carry the booty home. My mother had no idea about my father's stealing, I lied every time she asked me about all this shopping after hours . . . She'd learned to live with my father's arbitrary ways and didn't insist on knowing where it came from. My mother and I disliked my father. With that background I should have developed talents similar to my father's, but no way, I take after my mother. From her I learned to hate stealing, just as much as I'd hated myself for lying so often. My mother's well aware of my lies . . . God grant she forgives me!' The moment God burst into his soliloquy, the chief of the Gendarmerie looked away, fixing his eyes on a painful memory behind the desk, on the floor.

'This isn't the best place for a confession, is it? We'd be better off in a bar . . But no matter, I was anxious to calm your fears. I have no excuse for living off other people; as you can imagine, my salary's quite enough for me. I'll pay for my meat, sugar, semolina, and no coffee on the house! Another beer?' He opened a Pils without waiting for a reply. 'Please forget this shameful part of my private life and let your customers know the rest. On that condition,' the ironic smile returned to his face, 'I'll turn a blind eye to the insulting of an officer in your shop. The intention was clear. Do we agree?'

'Yes, yes,' I said, suddenly realising the strangeness of the situation. I was in a police station listening, paradoxically, to an officer putting himself through an interrogation and a confession in front of a perfect stranger. Bizarrely, I started to think that our second meeting should have happened somewhere else: in the butcher's shop, with my friends Arratt and Kaici.

Which was precisely what happened. Sayad became a loyal customer and a regular in the butcher's shop at those times when criminals and thieves took a rest. He said himself that Lattifia was a paradise for gendarmes – they were bored stiff – the only trouble came from a couple of lunatics, crazy old men who wandered the village streets, all day long, summer and winter too. No one dared approach them, it was always problematic making them board the car to Blida for their summer holiday; people feared the heat would go to their heads.

'Now that everything is straight between us, we can exchange names. My name is Sayad,' he said.

'I am Chafra Elgataâ,' I said, miming cutting meat with a cleaver, in a conceptually precise, clean gesture.

'I refuse to use surnames. A surname diminishes a man.'

II

Unusually, Laid Touhami left his imposing house with its dressed stone walls before the call to the morning prayer. Not having prayed did not prey on his conscience or disturb his present obsessive anxiety; the years of struggle for national liberation had forged in him a particular liking for the meditative contemplation of the dawn, which had always preceded his long missions across the Ouarsenis massif, bearing messages from one group of resistance fighters to another, and often too from resistance fighters to their contacts in the villages. After praying, he would thank God that he was still alive, to continue his patriotic duty, and take to the road along paths whose routes he knew intimately from a mental map the product of exploration, cautious investigation, losing his way, solitary marches and the determination to get his messages through.

The choice of site for his house was not unconnected with those treks in the years of struggle; Laid Touhami had been left with a mania, you might say, for steep heights. He would spend hours perched on summits, his eye sweeping across the plains, hills, villages and douars[10] like a golden eagle surveying creation, a complete vision, made obligatory by the pair of mares supplied by the ALN.[11] From the house, built on bulldozed rocks that almost formed a length of paved avenue, Laid Touhami could take in Lattifia and its surroundings at a glance. He could clearly make out the white houses, the dark lines of the streets of Rouina and Elabadia, or the sparkling green meander of the Cheliff waters, a peaceful, reassuring trajectory over fertile lands. But there was no better earth than the long, red strip at the foot of the Temoulga. Everything grew there: fruit trees, wheat, barley. Everything thrived there: poultry, horses, mules, donkeys, cows, goats, rabbits. Everyone who lived there made the most of independence, no longer in fear of one day seeing their crops burned by enemy fires or their animals confiscated in the name of the law. Three low-cut stone walls and a screen of eucalyptus trees surrounded and protected Laid Touhami's land. The fourth side of the rectangle presented a windowless façade that could be seen from the village; on the opposite side, the windows of the house opened onto the mountainous barrier of the Temoulga.

Steady endurance over hundreds of miles, across mountains and valleys, had brought Laid Touhami another advantage: sturdy legs, with huge flat feet, as if the calcified blisters were forever attached to that part of his body. He called them his shovels. He needed neither car, cart nor bicycle and covered the distance between his house and the village without hurrying half an hour, a journey he would not hesitate to make several times in one day or night if need be. This particular day, a grave occurrence, now a week old, had turned him from his path towards the village; he instinctively took the mountain route, a vague certainty in his mind that his missing daughter had chosen the refuge of stony wilderness, scrubby mounds and natural hiding places, after his vain searches throughout Lattifia and all the douars and villages of the region; in other words, she could have taken to the hills, prompted by the stories he used to tell of his many missions. Might she have taken one of the routes he had described to her so many times? As before, he would travel miles and miles, to put his mind at rest, until nightfall if necessary.

10 *douars*   meaning nomadic camps or settlements
11 *ALN*   Armée de Libération Nationale

The big knob at the end of the walking stick, pockmarked with little bumps, bounced at random off the stones along the paths. Sometimes it chose a target, and then the blows would multiply, slow, hard, crushing, in answer to the relentless questions, repeated unto insanity, that hammered at the mind of Laid Touhami: 'Hafsa, my daughter, why did you leave? Didn't you have everything you wanted? We all loved you. Why dishonour us? What did we do? Your mother and your brothers spoiled you beyond measure.' He would walk on, scanning the sparse but sometimes dense vegetation in the breaking dawn. He shouted his daughter's name several times before he realised this was a sacrilegious act, something he had never been guilty of before. This more than anything was why he considered the colonial invasion blasphemous to natural harmony, a profanation of sacred places, a crime against peace, artificially created by men: wars were waged by city dwellers, with the open country and the mountains as their booty.

When, from the top of his lookout posts, he used to keep watch on the movements of enemy troops around Lattifia and the villages then known as Carnot and Lamartine, he could not help his eyes following the horses that galloped towards the Cheliff waters on the hottest days – and the view would suddenly alter as thick clouds of pestering black flies swarmed round the animals. It was a striking analogy for colonialism: insects invading a peaceful place, with the water, grass, land and mountains changed to putrefying matter. 'Hafsa has been made a victim, she'll come back home. We were all good to her.' Again he shouted his daughter's name, stopped, and heard his sacrilegious call weaken and fade out, far away from the mountain. Laid Touhami recalled the routine day-to-day events that had preceded his daughter's flight, and the facts stared him in the face: Hafsa had simply left home. The various theories offered by each family member and the close friends they had told all ended in the same conclusion, a dead-end that blocked understanding. Hafsa had made minute preparations for her departure. The day was particularly well-chosen: Laid Touhami and his wife were going down to the Lattifia baths for the last visit of the week. They had put soaps, towels and clean underwear in a shopping bag, she had taken her white haik[12] from the wardrobe, he had put on his kachabia, and both repeated the customary

12 *haik*, meaning woman's over-cloak

words: Hafsa could come with them if she liked and spend time with her friends or the neighbours, do some work in the orchard, or clean the house from top to bottom. She usually chose the last option, and wore herself out making the floor, walls, wardrobes and windows shine and doing the dirty washing until she was utterly exhausted, ending with a few moments' coffee break before her parents returned. However, she was familiar with their weekly ritual; they would visit the house of her father's friend, the village mayor, to taste a South American blend which arrived regularly from Algiers.

The void left by Zoulikha, who had been married less than a year, had made Laid Touhami and his wife more fond and indulgent towards Hafsa; the two sisters had been very close growing up, even from earliest childhood. Hafsa and Zoulikha both had plenty of good will and respect for their parents, but if one, Zoulikha, had responded favourably, and even hurriedly, to the marriage proposals from those people from Tacheta, Hafsa, for her part, had turned a deaf ear, kept her mouth firmly shut and no longer dared look her mother and father in the eye. It was almost a game of hide and seek, depending on who surprised the other in a moment of generosity or weakness. Towards nightfall, Hafsa would approach Laid Touhami with his equivalent of two pounds of meat. a large plate of steaming broad beans, seasoned simply with salt, or hot bissar[13] in winter, a habit she had adopted after her sister's marriage. Laid Touhami wasn't fooled, his daughter's tacit refusal subtly entered their relationship. She was trying to make him see that she did not want to be married, nor follow Zoulikha's example, who had left the Temoulga in tears, but happy to be setting up a home. After his first daughter's marriage, he had to welcome numerous visitors, some he knew and some he did not, for there remained the second daughter, and Hafsa became the chief feature of conversation. Laid Touhami was very attached to her. He did not show it in concrete ways but made sure that his responses to marriage proposals reached her through his wife, who reassured her daughter by passing on the men's intentions. Her father's were clear: she was still young, and fiercely opposed to any union not based on love.

The moral contribution of the armed struggle was just as important as physical endurance or sturdy legs. Laid Touhami had learned to respect

---

13 *bissar*: dried broad beans with spices and herbs: mashed

other people's judgments, so the speed of Zoulikha's consent astonished him. He wanted to stay out of his daughter's choice, or perhaps be the last resort before her final decision; still through his wife, he let her know there was no hurry. Between the outside world and his life in the Temoulga, he felt a kind of peace ruling his relations with men, a detachment from the immediate ambitions that his worried companions in arms used to raise in conversation. Had Laid Touhami lost his sense of duty? He dismissed their allegations; his new position recaptured the essence of the struggle, its moral significance. The former freedom fighters and the revolution, separated at the base like two sides of a triangle, would meet at the summit, which was history. They and he needed to take care that principles born in fire remained inviolate. This wakeful conscience seemed to his friends misplaced, a get out from the practical business of the world, a serious abdication. Amongst themselves they said that Hafsa's flight was a consequence of Laid Touhami's inexplicable change of heart. He was responsible in large part for his own dishonour, and his withdrawal to the Temoulga reflected a selfish concern, attending exclusively to his family and his invisible possessions.

As for him, he wondered if his wife had faithfully conveyed his words to their daughter. Hafsa might well have drawn different conclusions from his silence over the visitors comings and goings. She might have feared threats and dreaded a life with no right to speak or any freedom of movement. What she would have feared – a supervised existence – Laid Touhami had already witnessed in various ways. Hafsa suffered at the hands of her brothers, two idle fellows who behaved unreasonably and abused their authority over her. Whether busy or no she aggravated them, her presence made them aggressive; as a child they had beaten her, as an adult they imposed on her the restrictions that moulded the exemplary behaviour of women before they became wives.

When a film – or two, depending on the calculations of the visiting film distributor – did not keep them in Lattifia, Laid Touhami's sons preferred to spend their moments of full-time leisure close to home. They were mixed up with a gang of youths who monitored people by lurking at a distance among the houses scattered at the foot of the Temoulga, forming a people's militia from a war time which would not go away. The films projected onto the white walls of a disused garage – historical and violent like war in general – reminded the hundreds of spectators of the fragility of a first peace when armed rebel gangs imposed their own law where they saw fit, with no respect for central authority, or men grabbed other men's possessions, confusing free enterprise with anarchic adventure. Laid Touhami's sons had never forgotten the attempted rape, on two occasions, of their mother and their sister before and after the departure of the foreign soldiers, when they were off travelling with their father

Nothing escaped the two brothers' cyclops eye: they had arranged that one of them should always be near the family home when the other was away. But Hafsa managed to exploit their weakness one Thursday when posters announced an extra-long film show, with two big war films and a documentary on the Vietnam invasion; she heard her younger brother reporting the exciting news to the older boy. Her parents went down to the village, soon followed by her brothers. Left to herself, Hafsa came out of the house, sat on a rock and stared hard at the main road through Lattifia, a narrow glittering strip, as if to make sure it was still there. After that she did not waste a moment, quartering the rooms like a robot, looking for personal effects, money and photos. The artificial light felt strangely inadequate, so she opened all the windows and pulled back the curtains. All the windows looked out on the high wall of the Temoulga, looming close, a view she was to remember for years, the only landscape in her life.

She remembered her sister's escape plans. Zoulikha had intended patiently digging a tunnel through the mountain, or steps all the way to the top; from there they would see the world beyond the douar. One day the two girls ran away when the men were out. Their mother turned a blind eye when, one afternoon, they ventured into the Temoulga, hoping to find the cave they had explored years earlier with their father, who had been proud to show them a trace of his heroic past, the refuge for war-weary resistance fighters. For ages Hafsa and Zoulikha searched in vain for the entrance to the cave, until they were on the point of returning home, for the men would not be late back, their father would be tired of arguing and swigging cups of tasteless coffee, their brothers stuffed to bursting with violent images. Then Zoulikha saw some rusty tins and an army boot with a hole in the sole and uttered a cry of joy: the cavern was close by. The two sisters were afraid to go in through the narrow opening; Zoulikha stuck her head in and pulled it straight out, frightened by the darkness. In her mind's eye, Hafsa sketched a map of where the cave was, engraving on her memory the robust shrub emerging from a layer of small rocks to the left of the entrance, about twenty yards off, and the coppery bump to the right in the shape of a shoe, which she did not forget, due to a popular saying of the time: the size does not make the shoe, a sure way to remember the place. On the way home, the two sisters between them stored up the pointers that would lead to their father's refuge; one day, one of them would need a shelter, Hafsa told Zoulikha. The money was hidden in a suitcase placed under a wardrobe in her parents' bedroom, a small wad of different notes. It was her mother's suitcase. Hafsa took from it a sum approximately equal to the price of a train ticket from Lasnam to Oran; her own savings would be enough to buy food. Her mother kept coins and other bits and pieces in a knotted scarf. She opened it and took a passport photo that was rolled up inside a tube. She remembered the general hilarity the day her mother had faced a camera for the first time in her life. Of her father Hafsa could only find the photo on his identity card. She rummaged around in the wardrobe and found what she was looking for in a metal box in a whole lot of Laid Touhami's papers: his old French-Muslim identity card where he looked much younger. In her brothers' room there were two piles of photos in two drawers, one on top of the other. She thought of looking through them, but time was pressing and she chose a photo with the two boys together.

The first stage of the escape, leaving Lattifia without arousing suspicion, went off without a hitch. Hafsa took a path through the middle of a corn field which came out on the main road. There she had only to raise her arm once, the car that stopped was new and spacious. The driver's accent differed from the Lattifia men's. He was kind and spoke slowly, saying he had been working abroad and had come home for a short holiday and to take care of property inherited from his father. He also said he was heading for Oran, where he was born, and asked Hafsa if she knew the city. When she answered no, he added that it would be a pleasure to show her round. She accepted. Later in the journey, he politely insisted on asking her to supper with him. Hafsa travelled in comfort from Lattifia to Oran, and had supper with the man in Mostaganem – a meal of fish and seafood – and it was the absence of the usual lamb or beef, that reminded her of her childhood friend, the butcher's son.

He lived nearby. The symbolic trade between them had gone on for months. She would allow him to touch a part of her body, and he would promise her two pounds of lamb or veal each time. He would say 'Flesh for flesh' and she would insult him: 'You dirty butcher! Go make yourself some offal soup'. But he was a friend, and the only boy she had known. The memory of him persisted throughout the meal, and she practically found herself saying 'flesh for flesh' when the man's leg repeatedly brushed against hers under the table. Hafsa summoned up memories of her friend to escape the heavy, new atmosphere of the place, a restaurant where everything was so clean it shone, and they served the dishes in funny ways. She wore her haik on her shoulders among women who were not wearing the veil, but it did not seem to bother the kind man. They ate together again at his home when they arrived in Oran, a light meal, when night had fallen and all was black. Hafsa drank a kind of lemonade she'd never tasted before, a flavour of honey and mint and something else she could not identify, then the man had her try another, which tasted better, then a third. He began to fill the glass to the brim Hafsa felt her body float as he helped her up from the table, her mind struggled to string two thoughts together, colours flowed into each other before her eyes, from the armchairs, the furniture, the curtains, the bulbs behind the fabric of lampshades. She thought she was sitting down in an armchair, but he lay her on her back on the bed. Hafsa closed her eyes. Naked beside her, the man asked her her name, and she answered: 'They call me, Touhamya, Touhamya.'

Laid Touhami had discovered the cave one day as he was pursuing an impudent snake, a harmless, particularly long grass snake. The time spent tracking the reptile was not entirely wasted, for after all, the friend the snake was meant for was working for the same cause in his own way.

In Lattifia there lived a legendary character, the stories he told changed according to the souq. He was a meddah and snake-charmer by profession, an activity tolerated by the colonial authorities, who held charlatans, healers, clairvoyants, tolba[14] and marabouts in higher esteem. His tales drew large crowds, fascinated by their circumvolutions. Laid Touhami's friend the meddah and snake charmer was called Teguia Elhess. He had such a craze for complicating even the simplest of his stories that

14 *tolba* beggar

they seemed to have neither beginning, middle, nor end, still less any narrative thread. His characters were kings, poor people and heroes. He distinguished himself from the other meddahs by not calling on the services of a flute-player, and he did not people his tales with witches, monsters or one-eyed giants. The flute-player's role was to keep the audience awake, to stave off the moments when boredom and fatigue overtook minds and bodies. Teguia Elhess had a trick, a masterly technique for keeping people rooted to the spot. Inside a box, a copy of a shoe-shiner's box, he would place a snake; circling around it he would tell his tales. At calculated intervals – for example the distant, heavy look in the eyes of a few onlookers – he would utter a cry and bring out the snake, rolling it around his arms or neck, or slipping it into his pockets. The effect was immediate and electrifying. Necks were craned, a shiver ran through the audience. The Front made use of his stories for less distracting ends – rare were the police informers who could make out their political messages or allusions to the realities of war, conveyed through the storyteller's lips. Chasing the grass snake was no idle exercise; Laid Touhami considered catching it just as important as his missions. Teguia Elhess had just lost his snake, it had died of old age.

Snakes were crossing the paths at a respectable distance in front of or behind him, like those animals who wait for a light to cross from one side of a road to the other; Laid Touhami had seen dozens slither by without really paying them attention. Occasionally, when the threat came too close, his stick would crush the snake's head with a sharp blow. He had followed the grass snake stubbornly. After several zigzags it made straight for the cave and disappeared inside. Hiding behind a rock, he waited patiently for it to emerge. Duty required him not to budge from this spot until the grass snake was captured. Teghuia Elhess needed it just as much as his comrades needed weapons. If the medium for the political message was to be reptilian, so much the better, he said to himself. Eventually it showed its oval head, some way from the entrance to the cave. Laid Touhami suddenly sprang up behind and pinned its head beneath the forked end of a long rough branch. Then he stuffed it into a jute sack which he carefully tied with a cord. Equipped with a torch, he returned to the Temoulga the next day and explored the cavern. Later he informed the freedom fighters of his discovery. After independence, challenged to prove his participation in the liberation struggle by his daughters' innocent questions, he brought Hafsa and Zoulikha to see the secret hiding-place. He went back there several times when his nostalgia for heights overcame him. The cave would be an ideal place to hide, that was what Laid Touhami was thinking that day; his mind was so preoccupied that he did not notice the danger close by.

The snake's triangular head reared up less than a yard to his right. The familiar rustle of the viper's movements alerted Laid Touhami and his reaction was like lightning – a reflex from his solitary missions, ever wary on stony paths. The stick fell on the animal, hit it between the eyes and crushed it to death. After a series of angry blows, the viper's body lay still. Laid Touhami breathed for a moment, sitting back on his heels. He tried to remember if his daughters had been afraid of the wild animals when he took them into the Temoulga. Maybe Hafsa would not have had the courage to return to the cave, or maybe she would have turned back, frightened by threatening noises. How could he know if she was brave or not, except through ordeals she would have faced *outside* the family home, out of her brothers' reach, or his. The cave was not far off now. With his stick Laid Touhami pushed the viper out of his sight and it was swallowed by the void. Then he wondered if his friend Teguia Elhess would be interested in a dead snake, it would be a good joke to tell him when he saw him, but he immediately forgot the idea of having a laugh at the meddah's expense: leaning over to watch the viper's fall, he saw it hit something with a human shape.

Wide-eyed, a sudden shudder running through his body, Laid Touhami stared down at the 'smile' carved from ear to ear in the throat of the man at the bottom of the slope. He recognised the face crawling with feasting insects. The mayor of Lattifia lay there, horribly murdered.

Zineddine Ayachi had been informed of Hafsa's disappearance as soon as inquiries among the family circle in and around the village turned up no trace. He had assured Laid Touhami of his complete availability and that of all the town hall employees. Almost every day he went to the foot of the Temoulga for news, spoke with his friend's sons when their father was not yet home, and visited his neighbours a little way off. Some hours before, as he was leaving his family to follow Hafsa into the mountain, Laid Touhami had learned from his wife that the mayor had come by the previous evening later than usual, around ten o'clock. He had been alone and on foot, instead of using the car. 'Nostalgia for the mountains,' Laid Touhami had told himself. 'He's as good a walker as I am.'

'The scum! They'll kill everyone. It's the plague of independence. A patriot and a mayor!' Laid Touhami was almost running, his hand clenched on the stick. In spite of their political differences, the two men had kept their friendship alive with frequent visits, verbal messages and gifts exchanged: Brazilian coffee for Laid Touhami and honey for Zineddine Ayachi. Sometimes, too, they would meet at hunting parties in the Ouarsenis mountains. The mayor's repeated offers had not prevailed against his friend's intended retirement. One after the other, Laid Touhami had refused every post he was offered. He considered his duty done and owed nothing to anyone, not the Party, not the communal assembly, nor the wilaya assembly. If these different authorities continued to plague him, he would take up arms once more to defend his peace, and rouse the peasants of the region too.

Zineddine Ayachi had persisted in trying to entrust him with responsibility for the problems of the youth population. Laid Touhami expressed his opinion on youth in a definitive manner a few moments after the inauguration of premises for the village's first football team. The mayor had shown him round, pointing out a magnificent rectangular plaque, more than two yards long, carrying the name of the club: 'The Lattifia Youth Members Sports Club'.

Laid Touhami had looked at the plaque in silence, then said, almost to himself: 'The Lattifia Sports Club for Small Members.'

The mayor smiled. From then on, he rarely mentioned the problems of youth to his friend. None the less, a common past linked them, an important slice of their lives, a knot that neither could sever.

The original reason for Laid Touhami's moving so far away was the wanted notice issued against him by the colonial gendarmerie after his disappearance into the Ouarsenis resistance movement: his leaders instructed him to operate in the wilaya of the Oran region, where he was introduced to Zineddine Ayachi and his cell of four men. His main task was to unmask and neutralise traitors and collaborators; the little troop judged and executed. Years later, Laid Touhami had come to the conclusion that in peacetime, the slowness of the law was a tragedy; in wartime, files did not sleep in their drawers. From the top of the western mountains, far from his family, he looked at the world with compassion, sheltered from its anxieties and contrivances, and if he sometimes endeavoured to look at a case again it was partly due to the corner the enemy had pushed him into; if a trial demanded an urgent decision, he would cancel his vote. His real participation in the struggle over that period amounted to a dozen snakes killed on the fighters' paths, a severe verdict he passed upon himself.

The dreadful 'smile' cut into the mayor's throat was the detail Laid Touhami repeated most often in his replies to the gendarmes. With the exception of just one man, the entire squad climbed into an four-wheel-drive, which was followed by an ambulance. Laid Touhami was asked many questions before they arrived in the Temoulga. He kept quiet about the reason for his being in the mountain. The cave was linked with Hafsa's disappearance and his personal problems, a secret side to his past; the mayor's death was a tragedy separate from his own. The gendarmes found a broad-bladed knife near the victim's corpse. Going through his pockets seemed to rule out the motive of theft, the chief of police counted sixteen one hundred dinar notes and three of five. He also found keys, a quill pen, an order book, and a bundle of printed forms with the mayoral letterhead and stamp. A quick inspection of the body revealed that Zineddine Ayachi had received a blow to the back of the head, or several, judging from the extent of the injuries.

The ambulance returned to the village, carrying the dead man and the gendarmes. The four-wheel-drive made for Laid Touhami's house, where the chief of police questioned his wife and sons. They all had identical versions of the same event: the village mayor had drunk some coffee, talked to the boys and then left; it was after nightfall. They didn't know which way he had gone.

Laid Touhami halted his searches for Hafsa in the Temoulga the day he discovered the murder of his friend. That night he pondered the idea of a link between his daughter's disappearance and the mayor's death; the place where Zineddine Ayachi was killed had him seriously worried. He didn't want the gendarmes getting hold of his idea, for fear of disturbing his family's private life and the quiet of the mountain, his old principle, that the experience of nature could only be a solitary pursuit, still remained valid. He could just about tolerate the presence of other peasants like himself, or semi-peasants; if one day he had to fight to defend the peace a second time, their help would be welcome. That second war would not start with crude weapons like knives, daggers and catapults, but with guns. Laid Touhami knew that some men had rifles and pistols hidden away, captured from the enemy in individual actions, their entry tickets to the fight. Like them, he kept a small arsenal hidden in the ground, between two family tombs in the cemetery halfway to Lattifia. One thing led to another, one idea to the next, and he remembered a detail that had escaped the gendarmes. Emotion had overcome their sense of duty, unless of course they didn't know that Zineddine Ayachi had carried a pistol on him since the night he was shot at, just after his victory in the local elections. The mayor's gun had disappeared. Perhaps the reason for the crime was in this clue.

There were people who cherished the same plan as Laid Touhami, they dreamed of building a Great Wall of China between themselves and the city dwellers, a cordon of fire to save the countryside and the mountains. They dreamed of federal states, rural republics and urban republics of other desert people, linked by trade. This kind of approach would guarantee everyone's future. The mayor's murder, committed by someone from the city (Laid Touhami was sure of it), would have been unthinkable had there been frontiers clearly separating the two different worlds. Zineddine Ayachi would be alive amongst his own people. The two friends' meetings resembled a ritual that went back to the years of holy struggle when they would drink more cups of coffee than they could count to give them energy, a small vice Laid Touhami had contracted in the mountains and the mayor at a young age, since his father considered coffee an aphrodisiac and permanently wore a necklace of coffee beans round his neck.

In fact, coffee had been the cause of Zineddine Ayachi's flight into the Ouarsenis and his joining the ranks of the Front. One day an enemy unit invaded his house on a phony tip that he had been helping the rebels, provided by a local collaborator who was operating on a large scale for lack of specific names. His information targeted blocks of houses demarcated by roads and alleyways and numbered in sections. The soldiers surrounded Zineddine Ayachi's house some of them climbed onto the roof while others kicked the door in with their boots. Four men suddenly

150

landed in front of him as he sat in the yard. He stared in terror at the black jaws of the submachine guns. A finger pointed to the coffee pot beside him and a voice screamed: 'Who's been here? Where are the others?' The soldier seized the single cup and the coffee pot, which he overturned. The black sand of coffee grounds fell on Zineddine Ayachi's foot, and drips of coffee stained his white shirt in damp zigzags.

'It's me! It's me!' he said.

'This coffee pot is empty,' said the soldier.

'I drank it all, it was me,' said Zineddine Ayachi

'It must hold at least ten cups. You weren't alone! Where are the others?'

'There's only my family. I drink a lot of coffee. I can't help it.'

'You Arab donkey! You're going to show us what you can do.'

Zineddine Ayachi's wife put the coffee pot on the fire, half full of water. The soldier giving the orders filled it to the brim, then poured a packet of coffee into the boiling water. 'A man that fond of coffee must like it strong,' he said to Zineddine Ayachi's wife, who sensed her husband's imminent ordeal. All the soldiers gathered in the yard. None of them wanted to miss the spectacle of the man suffering the torture of the strong dose of coffee. They cleared out all there was to eat in the tiny kitchen. Zineddine Ayachi started on the first cup and answered questions about his amazing capacity to absorb an entire coffee pot with no damage to his physical and mental health. He was supposed to sip the thick black liquid slowly; disobeying orders cost him a rifle butt across the shoulders. His wife and children were shut up, sobbing, in a room. He tried downing the third cup in two gulps. The soldiers were in no hurry, they were just sorry they hadn't found any wine in the house – one of them said he thought grape juice flowed from the taps in a hot country, a paradise where vines were all that grew. The gulps of coffee fell heavily on Zineddine Ayachi's stomach, like tar soup. On the fifth cup a nauseous saliva filled his mouth, a gurgle rose from his guts, he tried to speed up the forced tasting, then a blow from the rifle butt across his back caused a retching that momentarily relieved his stomach.

'Swallow it,' said one of the soldiers, 'you can't waste all that coffee.' Zineddine Ayachi seized the coffee pot, lifted it into the air like a goatskin and let the contents pour into his wide open mouth. A coffee haemorrhage immediately spurted from his nose, prompted by the heavy butt of a gun right in the stomach. The soldiers then took him to the Lattifia barracks, where the torture continued: they made him drink saucepan after saucepan of coffee prepared with soapy water, this time with the aid of a funnel. His denials did little to alter Zineddine Ayachi's fate; the soldiers set about ridding him of his taste for coffee so long as he would not deliver the names of the men who shared it with him in his home. A possible way out of his ordeal crept into his mind in the brief moments of prayer afforded him by his executioners, for he sensed the end was near. The faces of those he loved, his friends and family, passed before his eyes, invoked silently, he asked each of them for forgiveness, forgiveness for his mistakes and his faults, his aberrations on this earth. In the end, Zineddine Ayachi arrived at the last name, his dead father's; helped by the combination of circumstances or the irony of fate, his thoughts returned by a curious path to the cause of his misfortune, and he remembered the coffee bean necklace his father used to wear round his neck.

'I'll tell you the truth,' he said. 'My coffee isn't really coffee at all. It's a mixture of burnt chick peas, black pepper, paprika and coffee. My father loved this drink, it was his secret recipe. It's an excellent aphrodisiac. A man becomes a bull with that coffee! The more cups, the more thrusts.'

Every time they met in the mountains, Laid Touhami would laugh at his friend's story. Neither he nor the other resistance fighters had any need of the magic potion Zineddine Ayachi had invented in a torture chamber: without women it would be a disaster. The enemy soldiers sent Zineddine Ayachi back to his house. He was to prepare five litres of his special coffee, which would multiply their orgasms with the fatmas.[15] The future mayor of Lattifia owed his salvation to a psychological trick: he instinctively knew that these foreigners, the masters of his country, would follow their orders but also their desire. A very short time was enough to say goodbye to his family; the torturers' credulity would not last long. Zineddine Ayachi had no illusions about the effect of his decoction, yet he was tempted to add a few fluid ounces of piss from his belly, swollen with the soapy coffee ingurgitated through the filter. On the Ouarsenis paths, he urinated symbolically on the enemy he would be fighting for years to come.

15 *fatma*   name given to servant during colonial occupation

III

Little by little I was leaving the world of childhood – if I had ever really known it, being, unusually, an only child – and entering adolescence as head of the family and owner of a butcher's shop, provided with a false liberty which would very soon have literally transformed my existence, In spite of myself, into a perfectly smooth tabula rasa, straight as a die, were it not for the vigilance of Arratt and Kaici.

My two best friends had followed the same path for different reasons, turning their backs on the chief concern of the time: a boundless confidence in the benefits of education. At least this was my impression but in fact it had a lot more to do with the cunning use of the metaphors of the time than with any sincere belief in a political wisdom which, according to the epic diagnoses of the historians, had been absent for centuries on end. I say impression, my dear readers, because from my butcher's shop I could only see the ones that made their way to school, college or the lycée, not those who left them – often for ever. The university students could be counted on one hand, besides, they were rarely seen in the village again. Of course, I noticed the host of small business ventures which sprang up through the efforts of those kept back a year at the lycée, but I attributed that to their parents' influence – many mouths to feed and few hands for work. What escaped me was the excellent choice these adolescents were making, the way they were able to anticipate how degrading education and its byways were to become: a labyrinth of betrayals, false promises, manipulation and cowardice. They deserted the ship of knowledge well before it sank.

Had I, today, to rank my regrets in life, school would probably come at the top of the list, yet if its absence dominated my adolescence, and were I to make a second list, it would come in the middle, and if the lists went on ad infinitum, everything would revolve around school, a focus that was endlessly rethought, reformulated and re-evaluated. There was the futile attempt to go back there the summer my grandmother died, but that was a passing phase, with no great repercussions for the symphony of ambitions of my post-independence days, but which had a curious consequence, a predilection for the pastures that stretched between Lattifia and Chouahla, where, at the douar, I attended lessons at the Qur'anic school.

Precise aims led my grandmother to visit us, four or five times a month on Friday evenings. She would come in order to scold my mother, who had opted for celibacy, to go over the whole issue at the same time as the house, to question her about the butchery, and to supply us with seasonal produce from her garden: Barbary coast figs, almonds, fruit, various herbs. . . She wore the veil like a scarf around her neck, it was long enough to be used to cover the fruit, heaped in a Moses basket which she intended me to explore. Then she would take my mother aside and begin a unilateral discussion of quite vast generalities from which little in life was excluded: the calm before the storm.

Grandmother proved very susceptible to my arguments. The Holy Scriptures, I said, took priority over everything, even the butcher's shop (she kept nodding, like an Indian confused by an effusion of thanks); if I was to begin to pray – at my age I was already late – knowledge of the verses of the Qur'an was necessary, and since in that respect I was enormously backward (she was horrified to learn that I knew only one sura by heart, Surat al-Fatiha), my grandmother decreed that I should spend the summer, at least a month, learning the Qur'an. She had not forgotten the reason for her visit that evening and added that if she had no rights in the matter of her daughter's future – a euphemism to indicate the umpteenth time she had had to suppress her fury – then she should have first say on mine, before my mother. My grandmother died soon after, but not before reiterating her earthly demands: marriage for my mother and an education for her grandson. My mother managed to evade the first deathbed promise, but gave me permission to learn as many of the Qur'anic verses as I could in a month.

It was a month of happiness. I would leave the house at cock crow, glad to escape the rituals of the butcher's shop: waiting for the meat delivery, cutting it up, carving, sharpening the knives and cleavers, gutting the animals, washing the block and the meat display table, then waiting again. I put the same enthusiasm into learning and reciting the verses of the Qur'an as when I had been forced to leave the village school; the other children and I would repeat the verses after the master and push out our chests like oarsmen carried by a boat over a calm and peaceful sea, rocked at particular moments by the master's verbal tempest, exhorting us by example to glorify the words of God in loud, clear voices. I often closed my eyes as if under water, becoming one with memory and reciting without interruption the verses that had exhausted me the previous night, first in front of my mother, who was doubtful of my thoroughness, then alone in my room. I should also say that I was older than most of the other pupils, and perhaps that was the reason for my pronounced aptitude for learning more quickly, a fact remarked upon by the master who was sorry to see me leave his class. He sent two messengers – an old man hunched with knowledge of the Holy Book, and a local official – to my mother to deliver a flattering message about how serious and hard-working I was, but they were defeated by arguments of widowhood, only son and man of the house.

'Your son will be an A'lim,[16] Madame, an A'lim – Sidi Cheikh says so,' the old man and the official said in unison when they visited my mother for the last time, a few moments before the door was brutally slammed in their faces, my mother not appreciating the botanical flattery and wandering eye of the official, who, forgetting my scholarly merits, poeticised his request with 'you have the scent of the orchard', his glance focused rather too low for an innocent conversation-starter. The hunch-back fulminated against his companion, accusing him of scuppering the future of an A'lim and swearing to report everything to the master.

From my room where I was straining to hear, anxious to know the outcome of the visit, I heard him stun the local official with the worst insult of the time: 'You can't expect much from a colonialist jailer, how is it you're still an official?' 'Messenger of the Devil !' he exclaimed, still furious, then calm was restored and I remember as I looked at the ceiling or what was above it, if it were possible for someone's destiny to be changed in an instant, in a conversation of a few words, in two seconds, by a glance or a verse of poetry composed on my mother's beauty. Then an image was impressed on me, a white blot which grew into the shape of a sheep, and I realised it was the protagonist of a real story about my childhood, told by my grandmother to my mother that summer, to remind her of my love of animals (the very same ones that get nervous near an abattoir) and the cruelty of having made a butcher of me, so hoping to influence her decision about the Qur'anic school. After the two messengers' disastrous mission, the truth was that I felt like a sheep being sent straight to the slaughter.

16 *A'lim*   meaning religious teacher

'Once upon a time,' grandmother had said to my mother, who was half amused and half irritated by the famous narrative introduction, 'there was a little boy and a sheep, which his father had bought for the Eid sacrifice. The sheep was shut in a yard for a week. On the first three days it ate a lot, but on the fourth, something bizarre happened. It began to bleat, louder and louder, imitating the other captive sheep in the neighbourhood. Remember! It was your child who restored its appetite, by staying close to it constantly, speaking to it softly, stroking it, and finally sitting astride it like a horse. But your son had eyes and ears, he realised the fate awaiting his friend and kept warning him: 'Run! Run! They're going to cut your throat.' You yourself saw him more than once, bent over, whispering the threats he was hearing into his friend's ear. He wept his body's tears the day the sheep's throat was slit. Shut in his room, he kept sobbing and repeating 'I warned him! I warned him!' Remember, too, how he chased your neighbour's son, who was his friend, from the house, because his father was to blame for the sheep's death. 'Don't come back to this house any more! Don't come back!' he shouted and pushed him away.'

NEWS UPDATE

A Digest of Press Reports from May 2000 to May 2001

MOROCCO

Interior Minister, Ahmed Midaoui, appeared in parliament on 10 May 2000 to answer a question that had been tabled against his predecessor two years ago. He declared that the Islamist leader, Abdessalame Yassine 'can come and go as he wishes'. Four days after this statement the guards who had previously enforced Yassine's house arrest were removed. Yassine first publicly appeared on the streets the following Friday to attend the midday prayers at the Ben Said mosque. His bodyguards calmed the enthusiasm of his supporters and at a press conference he declared that his Al-Adl wal-Ihsan group was a movement based on spiritual education not a political party. The same week the government banned his newspaper, his summer beach camps and a planned march near the Algerian border. Two independent papers that had been banned in April were allowed to publish again and two renowned journalists (Mustapha Aloui and Khalid Meshbal) who were being officially prosecuted in the courts were given a royal pardon on 27 May. This settling of internal differences allowed Mohammed VI, to proceed with his official visit to the USA with a clear human rights agenda.

The visit on the 20 June was an undoubted PR success. Time magazine labelled the young monarch, 'The King of Cool, the Beatles of Arabian royalty'. At an acceptance speech the young king declared, 'I have done my utmost to expand the scope of democracy, consolidate the state of law, believe and invest in the dignity of every citizen.'

In Morocco government forces cleared the UMT trade union offices of 400 unemployed graduates on a hunger strike since early June. They have demanded more government jobs as only 180,000 out of the 230,000 students that graduate each year can be absorbed by the state sector. This in itself has only been achieved after the Socialist-led government have increased social spending from 38% to 47% of the budget. After the banning of Al-Adl wal-Ihsan summer beach camps an unofficial camp in Mehdiya was forcibly disbanded on 2 July and forest camps disrupted by official displeasure. Yassine for his part has set about on a widespread tour of Moroccan towns after his house arrest ended in May. On another issue the Supreme Court squashed the five year sentence given to Adib, an army captain who had revealed a story of corruption in the army, to the French newspaper *Le Monde*. It was decided that the military tribunal was not competent to hear the case though it also appears that Adib still remains in jail. On the 20 August King Mohammed VI revealed that Morocco has at last struck oil. A small but useful oil field has been located at Talsinnt near the Algerian frontier which in three years time may be producing 270,000 barrels a day. The discovery seems to have been directly linked to last years reform of the oil exploration law which allowed foreign companies to keep up to 75% of the profits. Twenty other potential sites are currently being surveyed by a raft of foreign companies from Canada, France, Britain and the USA. The oil money may provide the muscle with which the young king can push through his modernisation programme. He has already promised to direct the new resources to agriculture and education. Another scheme is to employ many of the unemployed graduates in government funded Koranic schools, chipping away at both rural illiteracy and 'political Islam'. The oil will also help correct the balance of payment deficit by reversing the estimated $1 billion spent on energy imports.

TUNISIA

The official press agency reported a cross border attack by twenty Algerian guerillas with links to the GSPC group of Hassan Hattab on 17 May. Three Algerians were killed and two Tunisian soldiers wounded. Widespread publicity was given to this event despite the adverse effect it might have on the seasons tourism. The official press also reported that on 24 May Riad Ben Fadhel, a Tunisian journalist shot himself in the chest twice as he entered his car. Alternative reports speak of unidentified gunmen and link the shooting to the article he wrote three days before that counselled the President not to amend the constitution so that he could serve a fourth term in office when his third term expires in 2004. In October 1999, President Zine al-Abdine Ben Ali was elected with a 99.44% poll.

After the border attacks the process of returning passports to various Opposition figures was halted and their telephone lines were once again cut.

The Municipal elections saw the ruling Democratic Constitutional Rally receive 94% of the vote on an 84% turnout. Islamist parties are banned from competing and one of the licensed opposition parties, the Progressive Socialist Assembly, called for a boycott. On 28 May a 1,000 political prisoners, mostly Islamists, held in over 10 prisons, launched a hunger strike inspired by the Ben Brik affair.

On 7 June the liberal opposition leader, Moncef Marzouki, received his passport. On 22 June he met Tunisia's exiled Islamist leader, Rachid Ghannouchi, in London in an attempt to create a broad-based opposition alliance to the existing regime. 10 December was named as the date for a National Democratic Conference. It is the anniversary of the UN Declaration of Human Rights and the second anniversary of the 'National Commission for Liberty in Tunisia' which contains many of Tunisia's most outspoken and determined liberals.

FORMER SPANISH COLONY OF WESTERN SAHARA

After the failed 14 May meeting in London James Baker declared that the conflicting parties 'be prepared to consider and discuss other ways to achieve a durable and agreed resolution of their dispute'. The UN Security Council extended the MINURSCO peace keeping mission by another two months on 31 May. In the dispute over the entitlement to vote in the envisaged UN referendum over the status of the western Sahara, Morocco has filed 130,000 appeals, the Polisario less than 1,000. International supporters of the Polisario in the UN (seventy countries have recognised a Saharan government in exile) have an uphill struggle against the discreet support Morocco is able to gather from the US, France, Britain and Russia.

ALGERIA

President Abdelaziz Bouteflika paid a state visit to France on 14–17 June. He stepped out onto a 760 foot long red carpet and a personal welcome from the President Jacques Chirac. Aside from official meetings he paid homage to the 180,000 Algerians who had fought for France in the 1914–18 war, to the 26,000 who died as well as meeting with representatives of the French Jewish community and the Algerian community in France.

Decisions to reopen the French consulates in Oran and Annaba or to reintroduce direct Air France flights (cancelled after a December 1994 hijacking) were not achieved. In a goodwill gesture France cancelled 400 million francs of debt, about $58 million, though Algeria owes France a total debt of $3.36 billion.

At the end of June a visit by Algerian journalists and academics to Israel kicked up a row. The Algerian President denounced the trip as an 'act of violence', 'traitors to the sacred values of freedom' and 'an unforgivable misdeed' in a speech delivered to the Tunisian parliament. This violent language is in strong contrast to the Presidents own pragmatic dealings with Israel and the worldwide Jewish community. However he must have greatly enjoyed delivering, rather than receiving, such a stream of invective. Many of the journalists he attacked are old opponents from the years when he ran the Foreign Ministry in the old monolithic one party state.

LIBYA

5 September. Libya's African Unity Ministry accused the CIA and Mossad of murdering its ambassador to the Central African Republic. Awad Sanussi was shot by an unidentified gunman on Tuesday 29 August.

FROM AUGUST TO DECEMBER 2000

ALGERIA

There was a government reshuffle on 27 August by President Abdelaziz Bouteflika who has brought three of his old FLN colleagues back to power. Ali Benflis, lawyer and ex justice minister was made prime minister. A hard-line supporter of the old FLN ruling regime who has purged moderates from the party who had complained about the army's cancellation of elections in 1992. Most recently he helped organise Bouteflika's electoral campaign and then served as director of the presidential office. Two other former FLN comrades of Bouteflika promoted into the cabinet include Mohieddin Amimour (the new minister for information) and Abdelaziz Belkhadem (minister for foreign affairs). The new director of the president's office is no less than General Larbi

Belkheir, who as an ex-minister of the interior is believed to be one of the most powerful men in the country.

On the economic front, first the good news. The doubling of oil price since 1998 has greatly increased the Algerian government finances. The export of oil and gas is expected to bring in nearly US$20 billion this year. Inflation is down to 2.9% and the growth rate at 3%. However interest on the enormous pile of foreign debt still consumes at least a third of the value of all exports. A third of the active, urban labour force is considered to be unemployed which increases to 60% for those under thirty. In real terms the income of those in work has been effectively halved during the last ten years of civil war. The trade unions are rightly concerned that any privatisation of Algeria's monolithic state owned industries will only further aggravate this depressing scene. None of the funds offered by the World Bank or the European Union to speed up privatisation have been taken up. The one exception has been the deregularisation of Telecommunications from the state-run Post Office but this is due to the worldwide advances in mobile technology rather than from any political will. Big state financed projects, such as the upgrading of the water system for Algiers or a brand new Algiers airport, continue to dominate economic planning and attract the attention of competing foreign companies.

MOROCCO

Prime Minister Abderrahmane Youssoufi has cut the Moroccan cabinet down from 43 ministers to 33 on 6 September. He needs that many top posts to keep his political allies content. His centre-left government was forged with the backing of seven political parties and benefits from the support of the young King. Ten seats go to Youssoufi's own USFP party, eight are held by technocrats loyal to the palace – including the vital ministry of interior as well as justice and Islamic affairs. The old national-ist Istiqlal party has four ministers as does the liberal minded National Congress of Independents party. Lesser allies include the National Popular movement (three ministers) and the Socialism and Progress party (two ministers).

The government and the free press continues to purge the more corrupt members of the old regime though in the process even the political parties of the centre-left have been found to be touched with nepotism, dynastic politics and curious cross party deals. Two such figures from the Moroccan left, the socialist agriculture minister, Habib Malki, and the trade unionist, Mohammed Messari, have been dropped from power as their unwritten but close relationship with Driss Basri (the old minister of the interior) turned from golden asset to leaden embarrassment. No such charge has been placed against Youssef Tahiri, the energy minister who recently announced the discovery of oil in southeastern Morocco. His downfall is attributed to his enthusiastic, but it now appears unsubstantiated, assessment of the productivity of the Talsinnt well.

Morocco is pushing ahead with its long term aim of making the Western Sahara route the principal north-south artery that connects West Africa to the Maghreb. Making it possible to send goods down from Tangier to Lagos. Work has continued apace on the new motorway from Tangier to Kenitra (already linked up with the Rabat-Casablanca-Fez motorway). Meetings with Mauritania are proceeding to encourage completion of the road from the capital to the northern border. Senegal has promised to bridge the obstacle of the Senegal river.

All these long matured plans make it ever less likely that Morocco will consent to any surrender of her western Saharan territories. The young King even spoke to *Time* magazine that the Saharan dispute was an 'Algerian creation'. Other sources have begun to question exactly how many of the Polisario fighters were recruited from disaffected Tuareg from the central Sahara. The Moroccan foreign office continues in its efforts to persuade the 24 African states within the OAU to suspend their recognition of the Polisario's Sahrawi Arab Democratic Republic. The UN sponsored Morocco/Poliario talks in London and Geneva were widely considered to be a step backward.

As a corollary to these concerns Morocco is locked into an unlikely row with Qatar. The Gulf State of Qatar supports Al Jazeera, an exceptionally free-spoken Arabic language TV channel. It annoyed the late King Hassan II who never accepted the Qatari coup of 1995 when the present ruler dethroned his father. Indeed one Moroccan newspaper even carried a front page cartoon of a plump Gulf sheikh holding the severed head of an old man on a sword. It was captioned 'He who betrays his father will betray anyone.' As some form of retaliation the Qatari TV channel failed to cover Mohammed VI's visit to the USA but instead gave prominence to

Ramy, an ex army officer turned Islamist who is in exile in Scandinavia. The recent Qatari purchase of US$7.5 million worth of arms from Britain on behalf of Algeria may have just been a case of business as usual. Morocco however fears that this shipment will be used to re-arm the Polisario movement based on Tindouf.

LIBYA

Muammar Qadhafi is one of the few Arab and African leaders to understand the charm of the open road. He travels by motorised convoy, often seated in a white lorry bristling with telecommunications aerials. Tents, carpets and white plastic chairs are visibly bundled up in the vans of this road convoy escorted by his staff and security forces. He attended the OAU summit in Lome, on the Atlantic coast, by road and crossed the Libyan/Egyptian desert to attend the post intifida meeting at the Egyptian resort on the Red Sea.

At home he made his first official visit to Benghazi for 21 years in order to deliver the Revolution Day speech on 1 September. This four hour long unscripted, speech, was listened to by a crowd numbering tens of thousands as well as by King Abdullah of Jordan. It was for Arab ears, for no European journalists or diplomats were invited, but turned out to be remarkably moderate. The colonel spoke warmly of the old colonial enemy of Italy as Libya's best friend while the 100,000 Libyan Jews in Israel were invited home. Even the USA got a rhetorical blessing, 'Republican or Democrat, after Clinton there will be no more American Imperialism'.

This benign mood was further buoyed up by the Libyan organised release of Western hostages held in the Philippines later that month. The hostages were first flown to Tripoli before being publicly released.

JANUARY, FEBRUARY & MARCH 2001

ALGERIA

13 February French foreign minister Hubert Védrine paid a flying visit to Algiers, meeting President Abdelaziz Bouteflika and Foreign Minister Abdelaziz Belkhadem. It was the third ministerial delegation in less than a month. France has reopened her consulate in Annaba and in the last year almost a quarter of a million of visa's have been granted to Algerian's wishing to visit France. Relations between France and Algeria have an intensity that cannot be matched elsewhere. An open letter in *Le Monde* denounced the visit as part of France's 'complicity in crimes against humanity' and sited evidence from *The Dirty War*, a book by Habib Souaidia, a disaffected Algerian army officer. His claims that the Algerian army has used torture and assassination in its war against the Islamist guerillas, whilst deeply disturbing should surprise few professional observers of the conflict. Apart from its close cultural connections to the group of French trained officers now in key positions of command within the Algerian army, such as General Larbi Belkheir, it is difficult to detect that France has any guilt not shared by other western powers trading with Algeria. Though it is widely acknowledged that she has consistently muddled any attempt by diplomats of the European Union to investigate Algeria's human rights record.

The Army spokesman, the usually taciturn chief of staff, Lt General Mohammed Lamari, denounced Souaidia who he revealed had been released from prison in 1999 after a four year sentence for theft. Souaidia replied that it had been a political sentence. More tellingly someone also authorised the release of an interview with an ex-emir of the GIA, Omar Chikhi, who spoke freely about his guerilla tactics. How his group of the GIA had targeted journalists, plotted the 1994 Air France hijack and the 1996 murder of six Trappist monks in order to break French support for the Algerian army. Omar Chikhi had accepted the pardon offered by President Bouteflika's Civil Concord though it is also clear that he had already 'broken' with the GIA chief Antar Zouabri.

Although the fighting is considered to have diminished in the last three years it is far from finished. It is claimed that their are still around a hundred domestic casualties a month. No foreigner has been killed since 1996 (although 120 died in the five years previous) so the death of four Russian employees of a state owned fertiliser plant in the forest of Eddough, near Annaba, in 8 January was a blow to government credibility. Indeed the month of a Ramadan saw a general upsurge in violence; eleven soldiers were ambushed in the east of the country, eighteen travellers were killed by armed men at a roadblock, sixteen students at a technical college in Medea were machine-gunned in their dormitory, the following day three families were slaughtered in their hamlet outside Tenes in western Algeria. By the end of the month the death roll was up to 250.

LIBYA

On Wednesday 31 January, after a nine-month trial, three Scottish judges sitting at Camp Zeist in the Netherlands found Abdelbaset Ali Mohmed Al Megrahi guilty of planting explosives on Pan Am flight 103 which exploded on the 12 December 1988, causing 270 deaths. His co-defendant Al Amin Khalifa Fhimah was aquitted. The British and US governments are pressing for compensation of around £480 million.

The prosecution's case was that Megrahi had tried, tested and then planted a bomb which he hid within a Toshiba 'Bombeat' cassette recorder packed into a bronze coloured Samsonite suitcase. This was loaded onto flight KM 180 from Malta to Frankfurt from where it was routinely forwarded into the hold of the Boeing 747 Heathrow to New York flight. The bomb exploded at around 7 p.m. at 31,000 feet over the Scottish town of Lockerbie.

A key item of evidence was Megrahi's identification by a Maltese witness, Tony Gauci, as buying the clothing which forensic experts believe was packed around the bomb in the lethal suitcase. The judges also accepted evidence that Megrahi was a member of the Libyan Intelligence Services, a cousin of one of its leading officers (Sa'id Rashid) and that his job as chief of Libyan Arab Airlines security in Malta was cover. They accepted evidence that two months before the Lockerbie bombing Megrahi had been involved in a similar operation in Chad. They also accepted that the bomb had been operated by an electronic timer manufactured by Mebo, a Swiss company and that in 1985 the Libyan Intelligence Services had purchased twenty such timers from Mebo.

The judicial decision was achieved after 85 days of evidence, it collected 10,000 pages of evidence and consumed £60 million. It has silenced many of the theories that have circulated around the Lockerbie affair. The trial judges found no evidence of Syrian, Palestinian, Iranian or Lebanese involvement and decided that it was an entirely Libyan affair that was believed to be in retaliation for Ronald Reagan's attack on Tripoli in April 1986.

One of the most persistent rumours had been that it was in revenge for the destruction of Iran Air flight 655 on 3 July 1988 by the US cruiser Vincennes. This was widely reported to be an accident, the large civilian Airbus aircraft having been confused by the US navy for a slim F-14 fighter. However Ronald Reagan's decision to award the captain of the Vincennes with a naval decoration, rather than a reprimand, inextricably confused the world's perception of this tragic event.

The Libyan government denies the truth of the judicial decision. The day after the trail Colonel Qadhaffi greeted the acquitted man, promised to disclose new evidence in three days time but then failed to deliver any hard facts in the subsequent three hour speech.

However impartial observers have pinpointed two areas of weakness in the prosecution case. Firstly Tony Gauci identified Megrahi as 'resembling the man who brought them' but consistently refused to conclusively identify Megrahi as the customer. Secondly they have failed to explain exactly how the suitcase once it arrived at Frankfurt from Malta, failed to be identified by all the various X-ray and security devices between arrival at Frankfurt, departure from Frankfurt, check in and re-packing at Heathrow. This is all the more intriguing given that all US Embassies in Europe had been alerted to a high security risk since 3 December.

The US has continued its travel ban and unilateral sanctions against Libya. Britain, which reopened its embassy in 1999 (and which has already helped organise at least eight trade missions) seemed more open to a pragmatic solution. Privately the example of the Franco-Libyan deal, where the Libyan government paid compensation for the loss of a French aircraft over Niger airspace in 1988, without accepting responsibility, was sited as a possible way forward.

MOROCCO

On 20 December 35% of the state owned Maroc Telecom was sold to the French industrial giant, Vivendi, for $2.3 billion. It gives an enormous boost to the Treasury allowing finance minister Fathahallah Oualalou to spend $1 billion on creating 17,000 new jobs in the civil service, raise wages by 10% and cut petrol prices.

In the general euphoria of government spending only the most negative journalists continue to look into how President Chirac and palace insider André Azoulay's may have helped broker the deal. There are also rumours of French government loans which will allow the Moroccan army to purchase new equipment and concern that the control of public utilities will continue to fall into French hands. Harder facts also continue to emerge about the 'mislaying of $1.34 billion worth of loans' by a state bank, the Credit Immoblier et Hotelier. These loans, generously extended to all manner of politicians, officials and trade unionists, were part of the system of government perfected by the late interior minister of the late King. As a form of state priming of a new venture capitalist economy this State bank was a disaster. As an arm of government policy, whereby all the more disruptive elements of society were peacefully included into the Makhzen system, it was a considerable success.

The Moroccan press continues to delight in exposing more details of this system. There seems a general acceptance that exposure, judicial enquiry and resignation is enough. If it is not quite a witch hunt of the old regime it has also allowed the socialist-led government of Abderrahmane Youssoufi to pursue a quiet turn-around. Most of the old guard governors – the men who managed elections to the orders of the ministry of interior – have gone. Let us hope their successors will allow the growth of a free and fair democracy.

In September 1998, the British Foreign Office pledged that in the Moroccan-Polisario conflict we 'could not support one side or the other in the export of arms'. This pious declaration did not stop the same Foreign Office – only a year later – from giving the Royal Ordnance a licence to service thirty of the 105 mm guns that actually guard the 1,500km long sand walls of the Western Sahara. The British ambassador to Rabat, Anthony Layden, acting to defend this official position may have created a new tautology when he spoke of 'positive neutrality' – surely worthy of listing beside 'economical with the truth' as a classic example of Orwellian double-speak. Foreign minister Robin Cook spoke of receiving UN sanction for the deal, to the derision of his European colleagues. Those familiar with the illicit arms trading between England and Morocco in the sixteenth century will wonder why our ministers have failed to keep to Queen Elizabeth I's famous codicil that 'such matters were too complex and important to be committed to paper'.

TUNISIA

The government continues to crack down on Moncef Marzouki, Tunisia's leading human rights activist through the pliant medium of the law courts. Moncef, a university professor of medicine, was sentenced to a 12-month prison sentence for 'spreading false information with the aim of disturbing public order'. In 1994 he tried to contest the presidential elections and in 1998 he founded the National Council for Liberties of Tunisia.

APRIL, MAY AND JUNE 2001

ALGERIA

Ex defence minister General Nezzar was whisked expeditiously out of France after torture charges were filed against him in the French courts by some of his victims and their families. The contrast by which France protects her old allies, whatever the morality of the cause, is in contrast to Britain's clumsy handling of the Pinochet affair. Ten days of rioting from late April to early May in the Berber-speaking Kabylie mountains shattered illusions of peaceful settlement in the region. A surprising element was the crowd anger directed at the two Berber-based political parties, the Socialist Forces Front (FFS) and the Rally for Culture and Democracy (RCD). The riots were sparked off by the killing of a Kabyle youth while in the custody of the gendarmerie. The riots were suppressed with the death of another 42–60 young men by the riot police while hundreds were wounded.

A major demand was the withdrawal of the gendarmerie but other causes are the recognition of the Berber language and a general malaise against high unemployment, the contempt of the security services, lack of houses in this traditionally poor, proud and overcrowded mountain district.

In Algiers the FFS and RCD tried to recover their position and authority amongst the people by organising peaceful demonstrations against the brutality of the government reaction. Crowds of over 10,000 came out onto the streets for both of the rival parties. They also broke their relationship with the government, calling for reforms and resigning from posts. However the Berber parties, traditionally secularist and opposed to the intense Arabisation of the Islamists have always tended to be manipulated by the central government come election time and then forgotten.

President Abdelaziz Bouteflika put out an address for calm on 30 April and returned to the theme again on 27 May. The role of Thamazighth (the Berber language) would have to be looked at when it came to a revision of the constitution but for the moment he proposed a commission of enquiry which would be chaired by Dr Mohand Issaad, a prominent Kabylie lawyer. Previous commissions of inquiry (like that into electoral fraud and the 'assassination' of President Boudiaf in 1992) have served only to whitewash government crimes.

The local reaction has been extraordinary. The Arsh, or traditional mountain cantons formed of groups of neighbouring villages, have revived as a unit of local conciliar government. On 21 May the Aarush (plural for Arsh) organised a 500,000 strong demonstration, with the villagers marching by in the neat ranks of their Arsh. Further demonstrations continued throughout May.

LIBYA

The formal written appeal against the Lockerbie conviction of Abdel Basset al-Megrahi has been delayed. On 2 May the courts allowed a further extension of six weeks (until 13 June) for the defence to lodge their written appeal.

The Scottish defence team are working on a number of briefs: looking at evidence of the supposed position of the bomb in the suitcase, position of the case in the luggage container, any errors from the judges and the fact that the defence team were not invited to attend the scientific reconstruction tests.

MOROCCO

Observers of Moroccan politics have always had to confess that the Democratic Parties, for all their external zeal often reveal internal workings remarkably similar to the authoritarian palace structure they oppose. How are the political parties responding to the new wind of change?

The USFP, the Socialist Union of Popular Forces, has managed to delay holding a public conference for ten years. When it came, in Casablanca this April it was refreshingly lively, 300 delegates marched out during the opening session and it was boycotted by six senior officials. The 77 year old party chief Youssoufi was lampooned but he got his way. He was formally elected leader (for the first time!), delayed the second congress until 2003 (after the next election) and got through an allocation of 20% of party posts for women. Opposition centred on such dominant trade union leaders as Noubir Amoui, protesting about being side-lined from the party. His CDT Union, especially strong in the civil service, healthcare and transport is a powerful adversary though the CDT – run on absolutist lines by Amoui – could itself be a tempting target for 'democratisation'.

A few days before the USFP congress the Moroccan Association of Human Rights held its 6th conference. Writs and court cases hang over many of the 350 delegates, most of these imposed for flaunting government bans on demonstrations. One of the more interesting court decisions recently made (on March 1st) was a three month jail sentence and a $200,000 fine imposed against the editor of *Le Journal* for defamation of character. *Le Journal* had accused the foreign minister, Mohammed Beneissa, of profiting from the sale of state-owned land. Another item on the Human Rights agenda is that of 'the disappeared'. There are over 5,000 cases or petitions lodged against the palace from the long reign of Hassan II. The speedy settlement of these cases on the South African model should be an urgent priority though presumably many of the actions of the security services have been buried while some historical events like collusion with Algeria in the forgotten border war of 1963 will presumably never be pardoned.

TUNISIA

The world financial community continues to praise Tunisia's hard-earned economic growth. She remains a model example, pasting up another year of sustained growth (5% achieved over each of the last five years). The IMF commended its 'strong economic performance . . . attributed to a combination of prudent macroeconomic policies'. Beneath the placid surface of the business community there is however a furious opposition to Ben Ali's authoritarian regime, divided roughly into two wings, the Tunis-based liberal intelligentsia and the Islamist exiles.

This opposition continues to manifest itself. Ninety-three prominent Tunisians (ex-government ministers and newspaper editors amongst them) signed a petition against spreading corruption and the prospect of the Constitution being amended to allow Ben Ali a fourth term in office.

The banned Islamist party, al-Nahda came a step closer to legitimacy by releasing a joint statement with the centre-left opposition party Movement Democratique Socialiste (MDS). The MDS party leader Mohammed Moada is however being persecuted by the government through the courts accused of defaming the state, brought on by his meeting with al-Nahda party leader Rashid Ghannouchi (in exile in London). Liberal institutions continue to receive a battering. The government having closed down the Tunisian League for Human Rights (LTDH) since November 2000 is now prosecuting its president Mokhtar Trifi through the courts. When the courts fail in their task of humiliating the opposition, the agents of the security forces take over. This was graphically illustrated when Khadija Cherif of the Tunisian Association of Democratic Women (ATFD) was manhandled on March 13th whilst she was leaving the courts. As ever the role of satellite television, and especially the freethinking Al-Jazeera channel based on Qatar, is now part of the political process. In April Al-Jazeera screened live interviews with such opposition figures as Sihem Ben Sidrine, Marzouki and Ghannouchi.

NOTICE-BOARD OF USEFUL ADDRESSES

BRITISH BASED SOCIETIES

The Society for Moroccan Studies, c/o SOAS (School of Oriental and African Studies), Thornhaugh Street, Russel Square, London WC1H OXG

The Maghreb Review (the only genuinely independent academic journal) and the Maghreb Bookshop are run by Mohammed Ben Madani, 45, Burton Street, London WC1H 9AL.

Society for Algerian Studies, part of the Centre for Near and Middle Eastern Studies, c/o SOAS (see above). Run by Sir Alan Munro and Dr Hugh Roberts.

The British-Moroccan Society, 35 Westminster Bridge Road, London SE1 7BJ. An active friendship club dominated by foreign office and press officers.

The Journal of North African Studies, a quarterly academic journal published by Frank Cass & Co. Ltd, Crown House, 47 Chase Side, London N14 5BP; edited by Professors George Joffé and John Entelis.

The Society for Libyan Studies (ex The Libya Exploration Society), c/o Institute of Archaeology, 31-34 Gordon Square, London WC1H OPY. Publish an annual journal, sponsor digs, the publication of archaeological reports, arrange an annual lecture program while membership also gives access to the SOAS library.

153 Club – the parish magazine for travellers interested in North Africa, the Sahara and West Africa. Issued four times a year in a bright yellow cover, backed up four or so meetings a year. Annual subscription of £10 to the membership secretary, Mike Foster, 4a Stonard Road, Palmers Green, London N13 4DP.

ASTENE, Association for the Study of Travel in Egypt and the Near East, 26 Millington Road, Cambridge CB3 9HP. Club for independent scholars, enthusiasts and academics interested in the history of travel. Busy four day conference organised every other year, publications and bulletins.

Centre of Near and Middle Eastern Studies, c/o SOAS, Univeristy of London, Thornhaugh Street, Russel Square, London WC1H OXG, tel 020-7898-4330, fax 020-7898-4329. Produces a listing magazine for all lectures, conferences and exhibitions including those with a pan-Islamic or North African theme.

INDEPENDENT TRAVEL AGENTS

For Algerian Sahara

Sahara Tec, The Sahara Travel and Exploration Company, Neville Farm, Lower Halstock Leigh, Halkstock, Nr, Yeovil, Somerset, BA22 9QU, e-mail 'saharatec@hotmail.com, website 'www.sahartec.com', tel 01935-891204.

Passing through Algiers there is a choice between the five 'secure' hotels that are routinely used by passing businessmen and consultants. Le Mercure, a 5-star and massive 400 room hotel is 7km outside Algiers and costs around £70 a night. The Sheraton, on the west side of Algiers, is around £90 a night or use The Hilton or Sofitel, in between the airport and central Algiers. To my mind all cede place to Al-Aurassi, the cheapest of the five grand hotels, the only one in central Algiers and with the best view. In the central Sahara use Mokhtar Bahedi and Claudia Abbt who run an auberge and travel agency: Tarahist, B.P. 287, Tamanrasset 10000, Algerie; tel/fax: 00213-2934 4671.

For Egypt and the Western Desert

Zarzora Expedition Team, e-mail 'info@zarzora.com' or 'www.zarzora.com'

For Libya

I have travelled with three good local travel agents:

Happy days, Winzrik and Wings who have provided help with visas, arranged hotels, transport, jeep convoys, tents, music, guides and restaurant bookings.

Happy Days Tourism Services Co, Misurata, Libya, tel 218-51-621907, fax 218-51-621908, e-mail, 'happydays128@hotmail.com' – ask for English and Italian speaking Omer el Nass.

Wings Tours, Tripoli, Libya, tel 218-21 333-1855, fax 333-0881

Winzrik Tourism Services, Tripoli, Libya, tel 218-21-333-6734, fax 333-8364

The British based specialist is Caravanserai Tours, 1–3 Love Lane, London SE18 6QT, tel 020-8855-6373, fax 020-8855-6370, e-mail 'info@caravanserai-tours.com'

For Mali

Affala Voyages Initiatives, Boite Postale 09 Kidal, Mali, tel 223-850090, e-mail 'cagbaye@aol.com' or at the capital Bamako, tel 223-210270. Specialists in the northern Saharan territories of Mali.

Tam Tam Tours, BPE 2495, Bamako, tel 223-430-439, fax 223-430-089, e-mail 'tamtamtours@cefib.com' for the attention of Fatim who understands English.

Two hotel suggestions for your first night in Mali

Mandé Hotel, Cité du Niger, Bamako, Mali, tel 223-211993, fax 223-21-19-96. Bar on stilts overlooks the Niger river, multi-racial guests around pool, effecient without becoming an exclusive, air-conditioned reservation.

L'Auberge, Segou, BP 400, Mali, tel 223-320145. Cold beers served in long bar in the entrance hall by Lebanese cousins who run the place. French cooking at tables in the garden (lots of ways to eat Niger perch), small pool, the natural stopping place east from the capital.

For Morocco

Best of Morocco, Seend Park, Seend, Wiltshire SN12 6NZ, tel 01380-828630. Run by Chris Lawrence.

CLM, Creative Leisure Management, First Floor, 69 Knightsbridge, London SW1X 7RA, tel 020-7235-0123. Run by Annie Austin.

For Sudan

I Viaggio di Maurizio Levi, Via Londonio, 4 – Milano, Italy, tel 02-34934528, fax 02-34934595, e-mail 'viaggilevi@libero.it'

174

For Tunisia

Wigmore Holidays, 9 Kingsway, London WC2B 6YF, tel 020-7836-4500 is the only upmarket agency specialising in Tunisia, run by Abdelkader Chelbi.

Medward Travel, 304, Old Brompton Road, London SW5 9JF, tel 020-373-4411 deals mostly in flights.

BRIEF BIOGRAPHIES OF THE CONTRIBUTORS

MOHAMMED BELMAHI

The forty-third Ambassador of the Kingdom of Morocco to Britain has a varied career. A Master of Architecture degree from Toulouse was followed by a Master of Urban Planning and a Master of Philosophy from New York University which led to a posting within the UN. Recalled to work in the Moroccan Ministry of Housing, then in the Prime Minister's office (1979) and in the Ministry of Tourism from 1982–88. Chairman of the vast ONA group from 1988–94 after which he was appointed Ambassador to India and Nepal and from there to the Court of St James.

HAMISH BROWN

Hamish Brown is a writer, traveller, lecturer and photographer based in Scotland with wide ranging interests in the history, culture and peoples of the lands he visits. Since 1965 he has spent several months every year exploring the Atlas mountains. In 1995 he made an end-to-end Atlas trek of 96 days, from Taza to Manri, and has used this as an excuse to write a book *The Mountains Look on Marrakech*, which describes much of the Atlas and Morocco generally. He has written or edited over twenty books, ranging from children's stories, short stories, poetry to classic mountaineering titles, for which he was awarded a D.Litt from St Andrews University in 1997 and most recently an MBE. He still organises and leads small exploratory treks and climbs, cultural tours and flower and birding trips in Morocco.

JAMIE BRUCE-LOCKHART

Jamie Bruce Lockhart is a Scot by birth and was brought up in northern England, educated at Sedbergh School, Yorkshire and St. John's College, Cambridge. He worked in banking in London and Paris, and as an economist in the Central Planning Office, Government of Fiji. In 1973 he joined the Diplomatic Service serving in London, Cyprus, Austria, Nigeria and Bonn. Since 1996 he has been the Secretary of the Roberts Centre, a private charitable trust sponsoring new initiatives in the field of democracy and good government. A landscape watercolourist who has held a number of one-man exhibitions at home and abroad since the late 1970s, his other interests include classical chamber music and sailing old boats fast. Jamie Bruce Lockhart began his biographical research on Hugh Clapperton (1788–1827) with an expedition to follow Clapperton's footsteps through Nigeria across country from Badagry on the Guinea Coast to Lake Chad. He edited a transcription of *Clapperton's diaries of his travels in Borno in 1823-4* (Koeppe, Cologne, 1996) and co-edited, with Dr John Wright, *Difficult & Dangerous Roads: Hugh Clapperton's Travels in Sahara & Fezzan 1822-1825* (Sickle Moon Books, London, 2000).

PETER CLARK

Dr Peter Clark, OBE, was born in Sheffield in 1939. He has worked for the British Council since 1967, mostly in North Africa and the Middle East, including a spell as Cultural Attache in Tunisia. He has written *Three Sudanese Battles* (1977), *Henry Hallam* (1982), *Marmaduke Pickthall: British Muslim* (1986) and has translated from the Arabic, Ismat Hasan Zulko's, *Karari: the Sudanese Account of the Battle of Omdurman* (1980). Married, with three sons and one stepdaughter, he is now a director of MECAS, Middle East Cultural Advisory Services.

'ABD AL-MAJID BIN JALLUN

Peter Clark's translation comes from the memoirs of the celebrated Moroccan diplomat (1919–81) whose elegant use of classical Arabic has led to comparisons with Tahar Hussein. His memoirs are now established as an educational text in Morocco. Although he was descended from a Marrakech family he was actually born in Casablanca and a large part of his childhood (from age five to nine) was spent in Manchester. He was part of widespread expatriate community that had settled in Manchester from the 1830s controlling the import of raw cotton (especially from the lands of the old Ottoman Empire) and the export of the finished clothe. At the height of the trade there were one hundred commercial cotton brokers in Manchester, many of the most powerful being either Muslim Moroccans or Christian Syrians. A century later there were only fifteen families left and many of these had had to diversify into trade in beeswax and specialist grasses. By the late 1930s the depression and Japanese competition had killed off even these and this cosmopolitan community was dispersed for ever.

BARRY COLE

Barry Cole is a city poet. He was born in 1936 in Balham, south London. Married with three grown-up daughters, he has lived for the past thirty-eight years at the Angel, Islington, in north London. Apart from two years (1970–2) as Northern Arts Fellow in Literature at the Universities of Durham and Newcastle-upon-Tyne, he worked until 1993 as an editor with the Central Office of Information, and is now a freelance editor and reviewer. He has published six collections of poetry and four novels. His poems can also be found in such authoritative anthologies as Penguin's *British Poetry Since 1945* and *The Oxford Book of Twentieth Century Verse*.

ANTHONY GLADSTONE-THOMPSON

'A Wedding in Fez' is taken from Anthony Gladstone-Thompson's forthcoming novel *Mauresque*. He is a traveller and writer living in London long devoted to Morocco, a passion shared by his wife who paints the landscapes of the Maghreb. Anthony first visited Morocco in 1964 but immersed himself more fully in the culture when he taught in Casablanca from 1966–73 where he first met his Moroccan born wife Janine.

JANE LOVELESS

Jane Loveless first visited Morocco in 1971 travelling with her textile-dealing husband, Clive Loveless and her two children. She returned many times but after the break-up of her marriage she moved permanently to Essaouira. Her enthusiastic support of the local gnawa musicians led to a number of foreign tours (like that of the London based Music Village) and eventually to the creation of the gnawa music festival in 1998.

MOHAMED MAGANI

Born in 1948 in El Attar, Algeria with degrees from the University of Algiers and the University of London. Works include *Histoire et Sociologie chez Ibn Khaldoun, An Icelandic Dream, Un Temps Berlinois, La Faille du Ciel* and *Esthétique de Boucher* from which Lulu Norman has made her translation

PETER MORRIS

Journalist, writer and financier. Peter Morris has a long relationship with Tunis and Tunisia fed by his research for writing the *Rough Guide to Tunisia*.

LULU NORMAN

Freelance translator in French, Arabic and English based in central London with a passionate concern for Maghnebi fiction.

BARNABY ROGERSON

Barnaby Rogerson is a writer, traveller and publisher based in London. He has written *The Travellers History of North Africa* and guide books to Morocco, Cyprus, Istanbul and Tunisia (with Rose Baring). He has also written a number of travel-articles on the Islamic countries of the Mediterranean for magazines and newspapers such as *Cornucopia, House and Garden*, the *Independent*, the *Evening Standard*, the *Art Quarterly* and the *Daily Telegraph*. With his partner he runs Sickle Moon and Eland Books which have reprinted over fifty of the greatest works of travel-literature.

DR ABDELHADI TAZI

Dr Abdelhadi Tazi is a scholar, traveller, historian and diplomat who has served as the Moroccan Ambassador to India. He was educated in the purely Arabic and Islamic environment of the ancient Karaouiyne university of Fez. Dr Abdelhadi Tazi has spent twelve years following the travels of Ibn Battuta, searching out references in the archives of local courts, colleges and libraries. Ibn Battuta was born in Tangier in 1304 and first started his travels as a young man taking the pilgrimage to Mecca. Twenty-five years later he returned home, having travelled across the length and breadth of the Islamic world, including service as a judge in

India and as a diplomat in China. He retired to Fez in 1354 where he dictated his travels to a young secretary which were to be supplemented by two further travels to Spain and across the Sahara to Mali. Dr Abdelhadi Tazi's five-volume study of Ibn Battuta has won wide acclaim. He is a Member of the Royal Academy of Morocco.

JOHN WRIGHT

Dr John Wright is a writer and broadcaster on Libya, energy affairs and the Arab world. He was born in London and educated at St Paul's School. His first introduction to the Arab world came when he served with the RAF in Iraq from 1957–8. For some years on the staff of a foreign news agency in London, in 1965 he joined the English language Sunday Ghibli newspaper in Tripoli from where he went to Italy to continue his studies on Libya. His books on Libya include *Libya* (1969), *Libya: A Modern History* (1982), *Libya, Chad and the Central Sahara* (1989) as well as co-editing *Difficult & Dangerous Roads: Hugh Clapperton's Travels in Sahara & Fezzan 1822–1825*.